DON'T HOLD BACK

DON'T
HOLD
BACK

Leaving Behind the American Gospel
to Follow Jesus Fully

DAVID PLATT

MULTNOMAH

Don't Hold Back

All Scripture quotations are taken from the ESV® Bible (The Holy Bible, English Standard Version®), copyright © 2001 by Crossway, a publishing ministry of Good News Publishers. Used by permission. All rights reserved.

Details in some anecdotes and stories have been changed to protect the identities of the persons involved.

The author's royalties from this book will go toward promoting the glory of Christ in all nations.

Published in the United States by Multnomah, an imprint of Random House, a division of Penguin Random House LLC.

MULTNOMAH® and its mountain colophon are registered trademarks of Penguin Random House LLC.

Published in association with Yates & Yates, www.yates2.com.

Hardback ISBN 978-0-7352-9144-7
Ebook ISBN 978-0-7352-9145-4

The Cataloging-in-Publication Data is on file with the Library of Congress.

Printed in Canada on acid-free paper

waterbrookmultnomah.com

9 8 7 6 5 4 3 2 1

First Edition

Book design by Diane Hobbing

SPECIAL SALES Most Multnomah books are available at special quantity discounts when purchased in bulk by corporations, organizations, and special-interest groups. Custom imprinting or excerpting can also be done to fit special needs. For information, please email specialmarketscms@penguinrandomhouse.com.

For discouraged, disillusioned, damaged,
doubting, and divided Christians,
and, most importantly, for the next generation,
who longs to see more of Christ.

THE GOSPEL

The gospel is the good news that the one and only true God, the loving Creator, sovereign King, and holy Judge of all, has looked on men and women wonderfully, equally, and uniquely made in his image who have rebelled against him, are separated from him, and deserve death before him, and he has sent his Son, Jesus, God in the flesh, to live a perfect and powerful life, to die a sacrificial and substitutionary death, and to rise from the grave in victory over sin, Satan, and death. The gospel is a gracious invitation from God for sinners from every nation, tribe, people, and language to repent and believe in Jesus for the forgiveness of their sins, turning from all idols to declare allegiance to Jesus alone as King and trust in Jesus alone as Lord. The gospel is a guarantee that Jesus will come again in glory to consummate his kingdom for the redeemed from every nation, tribe, people, and language in a new heaven and a new earth where all things will be made new in the light of his holy presence and where his perfect rule and reign will have no end. According to the gospel, all people who do not trust in Jesus will experience everlasting judgment from God, and all people who trust in Jesus will experience everlasting joy with God.

CONTENTS

INTRODUCTION

The Risk Before Us

"Are you willing to risk it all for this?"

Harry stared straight into my eyes as he asked the question. A follower of Jesus for decades longer than I have been alive, he wasn't wasting time on small talk. We sat at a small table in a reception room atop the Museum of the Bible in downtown Washington, D.C. Over Harry's shoulder, I could see the U.S. Capitol looming just blocks away.

My family and I had moved to metro Washington a few years prior, and I was walking through some of the most challenging and discouraging days I have ever experienced. Sure, criticism and opposition had come when I wrote a book a decade ago on the cost of following Jesus and taking back your faith from the American dream. But so had accolades and opportunities. Lots of them. The church I pastored at that time was growing, and I was invited to speak at all kinds of events in all kinds of places. In a strange twist, writing about spurning the American dream actually brought me many things we associate with that dream.

But the scene was different now. Our church, like so many others, was struggling through the effects of a global pandemic. Our city and country had experienced tumultuous days of elections, protests, and riots. Tension over politics and race was causing deep divisions, leaving torn and tattered families and churches in its wake. I was still preaching about what it means to follow Jesus, but this time, I wasn't receiving accolades. Instead, my character was being attacked, my name was being slandered, my love for God and devotion to his Word were being questioned, and our church was being sued as part of an effort by a few people to oust our pastors (including me). I was weary and at the end of my rope.

Harry knew all this. He'd heard the rumors and seen the headlines. And after many conversations with pastors in similar situations around the country, he also knew our church family wasn't alone.

"You've had a good reputation with a comfortable job in a large church," he said. "Are you willing to risk it all for this?"

Silence sat at our table for a moment.

Harry looked to the side and began telling a story about a pastor friend of his who, many years before, walked through significant challenges in his church. Many in his congregation had accused him of being too "this" or not enough "that," and eventually the pastor made a fateful decision. In Harry's words, "He decided that the applause of people was more important to him than faithfulness to God." So the pastor changed course. To avert criticism, he gave in. He bent over backward to appease people, protect his reputation, and keep his position in the church.

"And it worked," Harry said. "The pastor was able to stay, and the people were pleased. But in the end," Harry continued, "he lost something irreplaceable from his ministry and, more importantly, his life. Deep down, he knew he wasn't willing to pay the price that conviction requires."

Harry fixed his gaze on me and said gently, "Press on, and don't hold back."

After a pause, he asked if he could pray for me.

"I would appreciate that," I said quietly.

We bowed our heads as Harry prayed for courage to press on, for grace to love the church and lead people to Jesus, and for God's help in it all.

—

I'm writing this book because I don't believe Harry's words were just for me. I know I'm not alone when it comes to discouragement, frustration, and weariness as a follower of Jesus during these days. From my point of view at the epicenter of my country, I see carnage on all sides among Christians. Individuals who've experienced spiritual, emotional, relational, and even physical hurt in the church. Families strained and friends no longer on speaking terms. Elder boards split into enemy camps. Denominations being hijacked by one heated faction or another. Longtime church members walking away in disgust. Many Christians distancing themselves from the church, and scores of young adults, college students, and teenagers disengaging from the church altogether. And so much of this, mind you, has so little to do with the message of Jesus or God's saving grace for our world.

The effects in the church have been devastating. I know and hear from so many Christians who feel disillusioned or damaged by the church. Many are experiencing doubts about the church and in some cases about Jesus himself. In my darker moments, I am one of those Christians.

Each of our journeys to this moment is unique. Yet we find ourselves together in a historic struggle that is social, political, spiritual, and personal all at the same time. We've been turned off by the politics of the church or turned away by a lack of compassion in the church. We've witnessed scandals among church leaders or even endured sexual abuse by them. We've watched the preservation of long-standing institutions and the promotion of high-profile personalities trump compassion for hurting people. We've scrolled through endless slander on social media and become addicted to attacks between supposed Christian brothers and sisters. In it all, we've seen the viruses of pride, self-promotion, and lust for power infect not just our country but our church.

Add to these dynamics the apathy and complacency that already existed in cultural Christianity, and we find ourselves looking around on a Sunday morning and wondering, *Isn't there more to Jesus than this? Isn't there more to the church than this?*

And I'm writing this book to say, *There is.*

There is so much more to Jesus and so much more to the church than what you and I see in the world around us right now. And we can experience it. Better put, we can experience *him.* We can experience the awe-filled wonder of Jesus and the otherworldly beauty of his church. But to do so, some things are going to have to be different. Starting not in "those people," but in you and me.

That leads to the title of this book. I mentioned how a decade ago I wrote about the need for Christians to take back our faith from the American dream. But years later, having moved to the capital of my country and having experienced up close and personal the unhealth of the American church, I've come to a clear conclusion: *The problem is not just an American dream that has consumed our lives but an American gospel that has hijacked our hearts.*

What do I mean by an *American* gospel?

For far too long, we have traded in the biblical gospel that exalts Jesus above everything in this world for an American gospel that prostitutes Jesus for the sake of comfort, power, politics, and prosperity in our country. The evidence is all around us. Instead of being eager to unite around the glory of Jesus, Christians are quick to divide over the idolatry of personal and political convictions. Instead of enjoying the multiethnic beauty Jesus has made possible for us in the church, Christians are still segregating by the color of our skin. Instead of sharing God's Word like it's water for thirsty friends in a spiritual desert, we're wielding it like it's a weapon against our enemies in a culture war. As followers of the just Ruler of the universe, we're ignoring rampant injustice around us, and we're so caught up in calls to promote the greatness of our nation that we're essentially disregarding Jesus's command to take the gospel to all nations.

In other words, so much of what we're experiencing in the church today—the discouragement, disillusionment, damage, doubt, and division—is a direct outcome of accepting a false gospel in our hearts. And if we would have the humility and courage to rediscover the true gospel, we could follow Jesus's lead into a different future.

A future of fighting for—not with—one another as brothers and sisters in Christ, realizing that the true gospel transforms walls of hostility into otherworldly unity.

A future that turns the tide on centuries of racial division in the church so that who we are reflects the beauty of who Jesus is.

A future in which we trust all of God's Word (including the hardest parts) with conviction while loving everyone around us (including those with whom we disagree) with compassion.

A future of doing justice instead of merely debating it.

A future in which we all play our part in bringing every nation of the world to enjoy and exalt Jesus.

Ultimately, a future in which we realize, either in a fresh way or for the first time, that the goal, gift, and prize of the true gospel is God himself—a future in which you and I find in him everything our souls desire.

To be clear, finding the American gospel wanting does *not* mean being ungrateful for God's grace in the United States of America. I am part of a church that includes women and men—some in uniform—who have made untold sacrifices to protect and promote the freedoms and opportunities we enjoy. Our church also includes individuals and families who have happily immigrated from countries where these freedoms and opportunities don't exist. You'll hear stories about several of these people in the pages ahead, and I'm profoundly grateful for all of them. More to the point, I'm profoundly grateful for the United States, a country in which we're allowed the freedom to practice, preach, and promote the gospel of Jesus Christ. This book is simply about charting a way forward that holds loosely to the ideals of a country that, however blessed, is destined to one day fall, and holds tightly to the gospel of a King who will never ever fail.

I don't presume to have all the answers. Nor do I presume that my own heart is totally disentangled from the faulty gospel I'm describing. I also don't promise that the road ahead will be easy for you or for me. From my own journey, I realize that enough destructive slander, frivolous lawsuits, and personal attacks will make anyone consider exiting the road altogether or at least slowing to a more safe and comfortable pace.

But in the end, I don't want to stop, and I don't want to coast. No matter what it costs, I don't want to compromise— not with the gospel of God. In other words, I don't want to hold back. Because I'm convinced that there is so much more to Jesus and his church than the American gospel could ever offer, and with you and countless others, I want to experience and enjoy him to the full.

DON'T HOLD BACK

1

FAMILY REIMAGINED

Coming Together Around Our Father's Table

I never could have dreamed how God would make me a father.

I have shared in different settings how my wife, Heather, and I struggled with infertility for many painful years. Believing that we couldn't have children biologically and that we were called to raise a family, we adopted our first son, Caleb, from Kazakhstan. Two weeks after returning home with Caleb and still adjusting to being parents, we found out, to our shock and surprise, that Heather was pregnant. Apparently what happens in Kazakhstan *doesn't* stay in Kazakhstan. Within nine months, Joshua was born, and we were a family of four.

The dream expanded when, three years later, we adopted our first daughter, Mara, from China. Three months after that adoption, again much to our astonishment, Heather was pregnant again. Our third son, Isaiah, came along soon thereafter, and we became a family of six.

Years later, Heather and I were joyfully content until a dinner date one night when the subject of adoption came up in conversation. We hadn't even planned on talking about adoption that night, but by the time we gave our waiter the check, we were in tears and smiling, believing God was leading us to adopt again. About a year later, we were matched with a child in an orphanage overseas whom we've named J.D., and for a number of reasons I won't go into here, we are still waiting to bring him home.

In the meantime, Heather and I were both reading Psalm 127 one day in our alone time with God, and we each sensed God calling us to bring another child, specifically a baby, into our home. So we started another adoption process, and months later we received information about a mom who was soon to give birth to a baby girl and desired to place her with a family for adoption. We were told that this birth mom already had a name picked out for her daughter, which was slightly disappointing because Heather and I had always said that if God gave us another girl, we would love to name her Mercy. But this obviously wasn't going to keep us from moving forward in this process, so we got to know this birth mom, and do you know what name she had chosen for her child?

Mercy.

This beautiful baby girl was two days old when she came into our care, and she officially became Mercy Platt as I was finishing writing this book.

When I sit down with my family for dinner, I think back to the times when Heather and I begged God for children and wondered if he would ever answer. Then I look around the table in awe and think, *I didn't even know to ask for this.* I never could have pictured this family portrait that God has painted.

Yet here at the outset of this book, I want to give you a glimpse of a family that is much larger, far more beautiful, and infinitely more unimaginable than my own. It's a family of sisters and brothers with different facial features and skin colors. They think differently. They live by different social norms. They come from different backgrounds and nations. If you were to see the people in this family assembled anywhere in the world—say on that field of dreams in Iowa or out on the Serengeti Plain—you'd think, *What on earth could such a wildly different bunch of people have in common?*

Imagine yourself around the dinner table with them in my country. See the faces of two Christian teenagers from wildly different church and cultural backgrounds, enjoying each other's company. See the believer from a predominantly Muslim country who recently became a U.S. citizen, talking to a Baptist war veteran who serves in law enforcement. Keep going around the table to a twenty-six-year-old Pentecostal social activist living in shared housing, laughing with a re-tired conservative Presbyterian lawyer. Sitting next to them is a Christian immigrant from Central America, just arrived with no documentation, who's passing the potatoes to a MAGA Facebook group leader who became a Christian in central Florida. What in the world could have drawn all these people together?

The answer to that question is the most important thing they could ever have in common. Each of them has the same heavenly Father. Each of them has been adopted by God through the gospel, and they've all been welcomed into his family as his sons and daughters. And out of the overflow of his surprising love for them, they possess a supernatural capacity to show surprising love to one another.

This family is called the church, and if you're a follower of Jesus, you're part of it. You're seated around the same table. And you're not just part of this family in the here and now. You and I will be part of God's family forever.

But today, before we reach eternity, we need to have an important family conversation. It's going to be difficult, but it needs to happen.

Are you ready?

Our church family is sick. Particularly the part of the family that makes its home in America.

Instead of enjoying one another's company at the table, encouraging one another, and loving one another in word and deed, we're caught up in a cultural climate that makes us quick to accuse, belittle, cancel, and distrust one another. Even more than being divided, so many sisters and brothers (i.e., so many of *us*) are hurting and feeling hurt by one another. So hurt, in fact, that many are leaving the table, while multitudes of outsiders see our table and want to get as far away as possible from it.

But, brothers and sisters, shouldn't we want to be made well? Shouldn't we long to experience what it means to be part of an unexplainably glad family before an unimaginably good Father?

"THAT THEY MAY BECOME PERFECTLY ONE"

Jesus is the master of unity, and he brought together a band of very different personalities to prove the point. In addition to calling uneducated fishermen—blue-collar types kept out of socially elite circles—he called Matthew, a wealthy tax collector who cared so little about political allegiance to his own country that he collected taxes for their Roman oppressors. On the other end of the spectrum, Jesus called Simon, a Zealot from an occasionally militant anti-government movement. Can you fathom it? Members of the extreme right and the extreme left—essentially political enemies—spending every waking moment with one another?

I'm sure it wasn't always easy, but it worked. They learned to put up with one another. They learned to lay down their lives for one another. This kind of togetherness is what Jesus wanted for them. Unity was his vision for their future. In fact, in his final prayer for them before dying on their behalf, he prayed that they would stick together and show the world a supernatural picture of his love (see John 17:20–26).

Ultimately, they did just that. They started the church, where the differences among new disciples only multiplied. They were women and men, rich and poor, young and old, slave and free, Hebrew and Hellenist. Gentiles started joining in droves, and Jews hated Gentiles. Yet once Jewish disciples truly met Jesus, everything changed. Paul, an ethnic Jew and by his own admission a Pharisee of Pharisees, spent his life loving and sacrificing for people he once abhorred.

In the end, ethnic Jews, wealthy Romans, and impoverished Gentiles from all kinds of pagan backgrounds were joined together in the family of God. Jesus had prayed that they would stick together, and they did. As a result, the message of the gospel spread throughout the world. That's why you and I are here today. And if we can model the way of those who've gone before us, if we can embody Jesus's prayer for unity today, then we'll play our part in passing on the gospel for generations to come.

Despite Jesus's prayer for unity, we've discovered all kinds of reasons to divide his family into opposing camps, and the emotional and spiritual fallout is proving ruinous. We'll talk more in the next chapter about how we divide into different churches based on the color of our skin. But we divide over more than skin color. We divide politically. Research shows that a majority of churchgoers prefer attending church with people who share their political views, and few attend services alongside people with different political opinions.[1] We divide theologically over differing views on spiritual gifts, the end times, modes of baptism, and leadership in the church. We divide stylistically over different perspectives on music, service length, church décor, and a plethora of other preferences.

To be clear, it's not necessarily bad to hold different views on these things. After all, I don't expect every Christian in metro Washington, D.C., to attend the church I serve, a church where we do things in a particular way based on particular convictions. I praise God for gospel-proclaiming, Bible-believing pastors and churches across our city (and around the country, for that matter) who do things differently based on different convictions, and I want them all to reach more people for Jesus. But just because we don't all attend the same church doesn't mean we can't all walk together in Christian unity.

So is there a way to be in genuine, caring, deep fellowship with people who are very different from us, just like we see in the Bible? I believe there is. Even when we have differing (and even opposing) opinions, preferences, and political views, there is a way to show supernatural love for Christians who might be quite different from us. There is a way to cultivate this kind of loving unity in our local congregations, in the broader church in our country, and in the body of Christ around the world.

And it starts with understanding who unites us, what's worth dividing over, and what's not.

Three Buckets

Picture three buckets with me. In the first bucket are clear, biblical beliefs and practices that unite all followers of Jesus. This bucket contains the gospel. To summarize, the gospel is

> the good news that the just and gracious Creator of the universe has looked on hopelessly sinful men and women and has sent his Son, Jesus, God in the flesh, to bear his judgment against sin on the cross and to show his power over sin in his resurrection so that anyone in any nation who turns from their sin and themselves and trusts in Jesus as Savior and Lord can be forgiven of their sin and reconciled to God for all of eternity.

The first bucket also contains the authority, inerrancy, and sufficiency of God's Word and includes the clear and direct truths and commands found therein. As we'll explore in an upcoming chapter, the Bible is the supreme and sufficient foundation for what we believe and how we live as followers of Jesus.

Christians divide from non-Christians over beliefs and practices that fall into this first bucket. For example, if someone says that Jesus isn't God, that salvation isn't by grace, or that Jesus didn't die on a cross and rise from the grave, then we should love and care for that person, but we can't worship with them, because they simply don't worship the same God or believe the same gospel. Likewise, if someone denies the authority and sufficiency of the Bible, then they aren't a follower of Jesus, and we don't unite with them in our faith. Instead, we love them as a non-Christian, and we give our lives to lead them to Jesus.

The second of our three buckets contains beliefs and practices that unite followers of Jesus who join together in a local church. This bucket includes things Christians might disagree about from one local church to another. For example, one church might believe that they should baptize babies, and another church might believe that they should baptize only believers in Christ. One church might believe that women and men should both be biblically affirmed as pastors, while another church might believe that only men should be biblically affirmed as pastors. One church might believe that God still gives the spiritual gifts of prophecy, tongues, and healing today, while another might believe that those gifts aren't as active in the church now as they were in the past. While Christians often divide into different churches and denominations based on beliefs and practices in this second bucket, they still celebrate one another as followers of Jesus and work together for the spread of the gospel in the world.

The third bucket contains beliefs and practices about which even Christians in the same local church disagree. Members of a local church might agree about baptism, spiritual gifts, and leadership in the church, but they might disagree about how the end times are going to unfold. They might disagree about political choices and a variety of other personal convictions. Even though these Christians might hold their convictions strongly, they choose not to divide into different churches based on those convictions.

Confusing the Buckets

Problems for unity in the church begin when we confuse these buckets and forget how to love people whose beliefs in any bucket are different from ours. Let me illustrate.

During recent elections in the United States, I heard many Christians and even church leaders say, "You cannot be a Christian and vote for _____," and they would put a candidate's name in the blank. Interestingly, I heard Christians from different sides of the aisle inserting different names into that sentence. This language catapulted a voting choice into the first bucket, inevitably leading Christians to question one another's faith because of the way they chose to vote. But surely opinions about who should be president of the United States aren't of the same importance as convictions about the essence of the gospel or the authority of God's Word.

One Sunday morning during the 2020 election cycle, I made an unintentionally provocative and surprisingly (at least to me) controversial statement. I told our church family, "We are not going to divide over [how you] vote here." I explained that if people thought we should divide over this issue, then this may not be the best church for them and perhaps they should be in a church that shares their conviction. I communicated that we would sincerely bless them as our brother or sister in Christ if they made that decision: "As long as that church is preaching the gospel, we don't begrudge you in any way. . . . We're not in competition with other Bible-believing, gospel-preaching churches in this city. We want to see all kinds of churches thriving for the spread of the gospel to people who need Jesus."[2] In other words, we decided to put the issue of how people vote in a presidential election in the third bucket—identifying it as an issue about which Christians in our church might disagree but over which we wouldn't divide. And just in case you're wondering, many of our members *passionately* disagreed on how to vote and still made the choice to remain united as a church.

Take a moment to picture the church family I was speaking to that Sunday morning. See a diverse and multiethnic gathering of people from more than one hundred countries. Looking out across their faces, I knew I had no hope of uniting them around third-bucket issues. And I was okay with that. Actually, I love that. Sure, it would be a lot easier if everybody believed everything I believe and preferred everything I prefer, but I don't have everything right, and my preferences aren't primary. I thank God for sisters and brothers in my life who love Jesus, believe the Bible, and sometimes come to different conclusions or have different desires than I do. These people stretch me, sharpen me, humble me, and challenge me to be more like Jesus.

The same is true in the wider church. I love being with sisters and brothers in Christ from other churches who differ on second-bucket issues. I get criticized for speaking at conferences or being in relationships with people who hold different theological views on second-bucket issues. But I can't imagine my life without friendship and partnership in the gospel with the broader body of Christ. I learn so much from other sisters and brothers, even (or especially) when some of our convictions differ.

In fact, just before writing this chapter, I returned from spending time with and speaking at events alongside two brothers in Christ who hold very different opinions on second-bucket issues. Still, I loved sitting around the table, enjoying meals, worshipping, praying, studying the Bible, and serving people in the name of Jesus with them. I came away from that time deeply challenged, uncomfortably stretched, and ultimately encouraged in Christ.

I'm convinced we're missing out on the countercultural wonder of what it means to be in the body of Christ if we aren't willing to kindly and respectfully disagree on third-bucket issues in our local churches and second-bucket issues in the broader church. It's time to learn how to hold firm to our personal convictions without compromising the unique and otherworldly unity Jesus has made possible for us in the gospel.

Carnivores and Vegetarians

Thankfully, this isn't the first time in history that followers of Jesus have struggled for unity, and God has given us guidance for the kind of conflict we're experiencing today. In the book of Romans, Paul wrote to a cosmopolitan church where followers of Jesus disagreed about everything from the food they ate to the holidays they celebrated. Specifically regarding food, some said, "It's okay to eat meat," while others said, "We should all be vegetarian." Division threatened to hobble the church, in part because different groups thought everyone should hold the same beliefs about second- and third-bucket issues.

How could they preserve their unity? Paul didn't tell them to create different churches, one for carnivores and one for vegetarians. That probably would have been easier, just as it might be easier for our church in metro D.C. to separate according to political perspectives or a number of other personal convictions. Instead, Paul called the church to build unity around Jesus. He called them to live "in such harmony with one another, in accord with *Christ Jesus,* that together you may with *one voice* glorify the God and Father of our *Lord Jesus Christ*" (15:5–6, emphasis added).

How do we do that? We focus on Jesus, and we clarify which buckets we're dealing with.

Paul told the church at Rome that these issues were important, particularly at the individual level, but they didn't determine whether someone was a Christian or whether people could be in the church together. It was possible to be a carnivore Christian, just as it was possible to be a vegetarian Christian, and it was possible (or, better put, it was *good*) for them both to be in the same church. Paul encouraged every person to follow their conscience—doing what they believed best honored Jesus according to his Word—and to love those who held different convictions on these kinds of issues. Read Paul's admonition in Romans 14:5–8 carefully:

> One person esteems one day as better than another, while another esteems all days alike. Each one should be fully convinced in his own mind. The one who observes the day, observes it in honor

of the Lord. The one who eats, eats in honor of the Lord, since he gives thanks to God, while the one who abstains, abstains in honor of the Lord and gives thanks to God. For none of us lives to himself, and none of us dies to himself. For if we live, we live to the Lord, and if we die, we die to the Lord. So then, whether we live or whether we die, we are the Lord's.

In other words, in matters where Christians are free to differ, individual believers are free to do whatever we believe best honors Jesus.

Look a little closer, though. Do you know what's really interesting in this passage? Paul wrote that it's good to have *strong* convictions about what we believe best honors Jesus, even in situations where we disagree with other Christians. This sounds counterintuitive, right? Since the aim in the church at Rome was unity around Jesus, we might expect Paul to have commanded, "Don't have strong convictions on issues of disagreement." Instead, he wrote the exact opposite: "Each one should be fully convinced in his own mind."

Fully convinced—a high standard.

God commands us to be convinced in our own minds that what we're doing best honors him. If that's abstaining from certain food, so be it. If that's eating certain food, so be it. Now, we might think that makes the problem worse, but it doesn't, so long as we follow the rest of God's Word.

When we're dealing with issues about which we're free to disagree as followers of Jesus, God our Father tells us to love one another as if we're family—"with brotherly affection" (Romans 12:10). We should welcome one another and refuse to despise or pass unbiblical judgment on one another simply because we might disagree on some non-essential issue (14:1–3). Why? Because we're "walking in love" for one another (verse 15).

What does walking in love look like? At the very least, it starts with actively listening to and seeking to understand one another. In the words of James 1:19, we should be "quick to hear, slow to speak, slow to anger." This command is particularly appropriate for us in a culture that entices us to share our thoughts and opinions through a screen instead of looking into the eyes of our brother or sister and listening in a spirit of love. A modern-day rendering of James 1:19 might say, "Be slow to snap, post, or tweet."

And just because we truly listen to one another doesn't mean we'll ultimately agree. But that's part of the beauty of Romans 14–15, because our Christian forebearers didn't agree either. After acknowledging differences of conviction, God tells his children that they have an "obligation to bear with" one another and to "please [our] neighbor for his good, to build him up" (15:1–2). What a worthy aim amid disagreements with brothers and sisters in Christ: to please and build up one another.

Let's be honest: There's a lot of attacking and tearing down these days, and it's coming from all sides. We demonize those who disagree with us, and we make reckless generalizations about and deliver sweeping condemnations of *those* people who *all* believe *that* craziness. Instead of having thoughtful discussions focused on listening first, we lob accusations like grenades. Instead of engaging in meaningful dialogue, we resort to personal ridicule. We have mastered the art of turning healthy disagreement into hateful disgust, and it leaves us damaged and divided. But this isn't the way of Jesus, and it doesn't honor our Father.

WHAT (OR WHO) MAKES US A FAMILY

In light of challenges to maintaining unity, some Christians conclude that we shouldn't discuss issues about which we disagree, believing such conversations only lead to further division.

But how can an issue divide us if it's not what unites us?

As part of an illustration I used one night during our family worship time, my wife, our kids, and I were sharing our favorite ice cream flavors. Of course, we're passionate about our flavors of choice. But would it make sense for us to avoid the topic of favorite ice cream flavors because it might lead to division? No, because having the same favorite ice cream flavor isn't what makes us a family.

In a similar way, it's possible for followers of Jesus to have different views on different issues—and discuss those differences—but still be a united church. Without question, our opinions or even convictions beyond what the Bible clearly and directly teaches about race, politics, or a number of other issues are far more important than ice cream preferences. But those opinions and convictions aren't what make us a family. Jesus makes us a family, which means that if we're allowing those opinions and convictions to divide us, then we're making them more important to us than Jesus himself.

Second- and third-bucket issues can't divide us if Jesus is the one who unites us.

Let's gladly come together, then, under Jesus, and let's not be afraid to discuss all sorts of issues even when they're difficult. Where we might have disagreement and division, let's strive to love one another well, just as Jesus loves us. And when we talk through our views with God's Word as our authority and God's grace in our hearts, let's be open to potential changes in our perspectives. Maybe more importantly, let's be open to the healing that our hearts—and others' hearts—might desperately need amid disagreement and division.

I think about responses I have heard from church members when we created avenues to discuss issues like race and justice. One Asian American sister wrote to thank me, saying,

> As an academic and social scientist who has been teaching on, and researching topics related to, race for over fifteen years in university settings, I am very comfortable having conversations around race and racism. However, what makes me discouraged or frustrated is that in the church, the place (i.e., the body of Christ) that is most central to my identity as a child of God, it seems rare or awkward (or deemed "divisive") to have these conversations. That is why I am so excited to have this opportunity to truly integrate our faith in the gospel around issues of justice and race.

A Latin American brother shared how he is often shut down when he tries to have genuine discussions about these matters, but he was thrilled to see the church tackling the conversation with God's Word at the center. One Caucasian church member summarized so much of the feedback I received:

> I am concerned that Christians, on average, don't have the skills to have a genuine, loving, humble conversation when we disagree with someone on a personal, emotional topic. I think this is a skill that we ought to develop, and we are not representing Christ well if we do not develop this skill of dealing with conflict and remaining united with those with whom we disagree.

Indeed, this certainly seems like a skill worth developing in our lives and in the church.

What might happen among Christians and churches in the United States if we made it a priority to gather around the table with other sisters and brothers in Christ and prayerfully and lovingly discuss topics on which we disagree, with our ears attuned to God's Spirit through God's Word? What might happen if we spent less time posting, commenting, and tweeting about one another and more time being with one another? What might happen if we had the courage to leave our echo chambers and listen to people who believe differently from us?

RECOVERING HUMILITY

If unity around Jesus is our aim and listening long and hard to those who are different from us is what we need, that will take a good measure of something that's fallen out of favor in American society: humility. After all, none of us has everything figured out, and we all have blind spots. Isn't it wise, then, to hear from sisters and brothers who have different convictions than we do and humbly ask whether there's something we can (or need to) learn from them?

Toward this end, let's come together to ask sincere and honest questions of one another, and let's carefully avoid unhelpful assumptions or unfair conclusions about one another. Let's intentionally resist the temptation to assemble and attack straw men.

In the tumult of the last couple of years, I had a sharp disagreement with a couple of people who I know are followers of Jesus. I was upset at them, and they were upset at me. Unfortunately, I found myself telling others about my frustration with *"these* people" who "actually believe *this"* and "had the nerve to do *that."* I was fully convinced in my own mind—and I was convincing others—that what they believed was wrong and what I believed was right.

But then something happened. I was convicted that we needed to sit down and talk. Thankfully, they were willing to talk with me, and as I asked them questions, I soon realized that I had misunderstood and mischaracterized their position. While I still disagreed with them, I knew I hadn't listened to them humbly or spoken about them appropriately. I apologized and did what I could to make things right, not only with them but also with others I had influenced concerning them. And I hope that they did the same concerning me.

It's frightening to see how easy it was to wall myself off from truly seeing, understanding, and receiving people with whom I disagreed. I hate it when others do this to me, yet I was so quick to castigate them instead of doing the hard work of honestly listening and humbly responding to their convictions. I readily admit my need for God's grace to grow in these ways.

Yet even in the middle of humble, honest conversations, we will still disagree on second- or third-bucket issues. And when we're dealing with second-bucket issues, we may find it best to be a part of different churches. But we can still relate to one another in a way that is very different from the world around us. By the power of God's grace in us, we can learn to handle our differences the way God commands us in his Word—with affection, sympathy, patience, kindness, gentleness, tenderness, and selflessness.

Forging unity in this way won't be easy. In fact, if my experience is any indication, it will be *really* hard. It requires a resolve to love one another in a way that is extremely countercultural in our country. It requires a commitment to live in peace with one another and protect one another despite passionate disagreements on some matters. But this kind of unity among believers is worth it. In a wearying world that is constantly beating us down, we all long for brothers and sisters who will stand with us and for us like we're family.

YOU ARE NOT ALONE

When I was in the ninth grade, I was invited to a high school basketball camp. Upon arriving, I soon learned that the seniors at camp traditionally initiated the freshmen in not-so-pleasant ways. I remember sitting with another freshman in our dorm room when a senior burst through the door, picked my friend up off the bed, carried him to the bathroom, stuck his head in the toilet, and flushed. My friend came back with a shocked look on his face and wet, swirled hair on his head.

I was next.

The same senior grabbed me by the arms and turned to take me to the initiation ceremony's flushing throne. But as he turned, another senior stepped into the room and said, "Stop! We can't take him!"

"Why not?" the guy holding me asked.

My newfound senior buddy said, "That's Platt's brother."

You see, I had a secret weapon growing up: my older brother, Steve. I was a runt, but Steve was a giant. Not only was he big, but he also knew how to use his size. He was the heavyweight wrestling champion in the state of Georgia, and during the championship match, he picked up and body-slammed his three-hundred-pound opponent. In our high school, Steve Platt was a living legend.

The guy holding me looked me up and down and said, "This is not Platt's brother. This is Platt's left leg!"

It was a fair assessment when you compare my size at the time with Steve's leg. And I don't think this guy meant his words to be a compliment. But I was proud to be "Platt's left leg" that day, particularly when my would-be swirler sighed, put me back down, and walked out of the room.

That wasn't the only time that being related to Steve proved particularly beneficial. On one cold winter day, I wore a prized possession to school—a new coat my grand-dad had given me. I set it down in the corner of the class-room at the beginning of the day and went back at the end of the day to find that it was gone. Someone had stolen it.

My dad came to pick us up from school, and when I told

him what had happened, he went in to talk with the principal. Meanwhile, I sat on a bench outside the principal's office. Steve noticed how upset I was and asked me what had happened. I told him, and he immediately responded, "Let me see what I can do."

While my dad talked with the principal, my older brother walked over to a guy who was the leader of a group known for petty theft. Steve pulled him aside and said, "My little brother's coat is gone, and I'm guessing you know who might have it. I'd like that coat back first thing in the morning; otherwise, you and I are going to have a talk."

The next morning, while sitting in my class, I looked out into the hall and saw Steve walking down the hallway. Guess what was in his hand?

Steve came to my desk, handed me my coat, and whispered in my ear, "David, no matter what happens to you, always know that your brother has your back."

Fast-forward a few more years to when Steve and I had both married and moved away from home. While I lived farther away, Steve still lived near Mom and Dad, and I'll never forget getting a call one night. I heard Steve's voice shaking on the other end of the line. He was at the hospital, where our dad, our best friend for all our lives, had been rushed to the emergency room following a heart attack. Steve could hardly get any words out, but three were unmistakable: "Dad is gone." We wept on the phone, and we promised to walk together through the grief ahead alongside our mom and other siblings.

This is what family is all about, right? It's about walking through a hard, wearying world together. It's about holding one another up and having one another's back. While it's not necessarily about body-slamming one another's opponents, it is about being one another's tender protector in a world that constantly tears us down.

Dear brother or sister in Christ, before our heavenly Father, I so badly and sincerely want to look you in the eye and simply say,

> I am in awe that I am in an eternal family with you, and I want you to know that I have your back. You are not alone. As your brother, I am with you. Even if we're not in the same local church and even if we have a variety of sharp disagreements about second- and third-bucket issues—actually, I would say that especially if we're in different churches with sharp disagreements—I am still for you. I genuinely love you.

At the same time, I want to honestly and humbly confess my need for you to look me in the eye and say the same thing back to me as your brother in Christ. God has wired us to need and want otherworldly family like this. As followers of Jesus, we share a supernatural bloodline that supersedes ethnic backgrounds, socioeconomic situations, political parties and positions, and personal preferences and opinions.

Despite all our differences, we are *one family* in Christ.

Our family is not fundamentally African American, Asian American, European American, Hispanic American, Native American, or even American. Our family is not fundamentally rich or poor. Our family is not fundamentally Republican, Democrat, or Independent. None of these things are grounds for division among us, because our family is fundamentally Christian. We are a chosen people, a royal priest-hood, a holy nation, and a people possessed by God himself (1 Peter 2:9). In the biblical gospel, we have been acquitted of sin before God the Judge and adopted as daughters and sons by God the Father. And if we will realize and constantly re-member this, we will experience so much needed healing not just in the church but in our lives.

2

FOLLOWING CHRIST IN MULTICOLOR

Embracing the Beauty of Ethnicity

I remember my first date with Heather like it was yesterday.

Stone Mountain Park, located a short ten minutes away from my childhood home, contains the largest exposed piece of granite in the world. Stone Mountain rises to an elevation of approximately 1,700 feet and is five miles in circumference. It's the most visited tourist site in the state of Georgia.

Every summer night, the park hosts a laser show. In the hours just before sunset, thousands of picnickers set up chairs and unfurl blankets on the lawn at the base of the mountain. When the sun sets and the first stars come out, music bursts through loudspeakers, and multicolored lasers shine on the side of the mountain, where three figures on horseback are carved nine stories tall and nineteen stories wide. It's the largest rock-relief artwork of its kind in the world.

Stone Mountain Park was the site of my first date in high school. Lounging on the lawn in a sea of people, looking up at the side of that mountain, I reached out and took Heather's hand for the first time, and the rest is history.

But what an ironic turn of phrase.

For all the personal history being made that night on the lawn in front of Stone Mountain, I was totally missing the larger history memorialized on the rock in front of me. Over the years, I'd seen the laser show and hiked to the granite mountaintop more times than I could count. This mountain served as a backdrop for so many hours of my life, yet I can't remember ever stopping to ask what it was all about. If I had, I would have discovered that this mountain—and the carving on its side—had been developed as a massive monument to racism.

Once owned by a member of the Ku Klux Klan, Stone Mountain was considered "*the* sacred site to members of the . . . Klan."[1] Years before I sat at the base of that mountain, people set up altars at the top, covered them with Confederate flags, read from the Bible, and burned crosses. They established this place as a memorial to the fight for White people's right to own Black slaves. That's why the three men carved in massive relief on the mountain are Confederate figures—Jefferson Davis, the president of the Confederate States, and Robert E. Lee and Stonewall Jackson, generals in the Confederate Army.

The primary planner and fundraiser for the relief sculpture, C. Helen Plane, was a charter member of the United Daughters of the Confederacy. In a letter to the sculptor, who was also closely connected to the Klan, Plane made her aims clear: "I feel that it is due to the Ku Klux Klan which saved us from Negro domination and carpet-bag rule, that it be immortalized on Stone Mountain."[2] Support for the granite carving increased with the rise of the civil rights movement, and Stone Mountain Park officially opened on April 14, 1965, one hundred years to the day after the assassination of Abraham Lincoln.[3]

Now, does any of this history lessen the love that started to grow that night I first held my wife's hand? No, not at all. Am I in any way guilty of participating in the Ku Klux Klan? No, I'm not. For that matter, am I guilty of owning slaves in the mid-1700s, fighting for slavery in the mid-1800s, or opposing civil rights in the mid-1900s? No.

But am I responsible for knowing the history of racism in America, for understanding how it is enshrined in the places around me, for recognizing how it influences people in my country, and for making sure that I don't repeat or preserve the harmful effects of the past, especially in the church? Yes, I am. And for most of my life, I haven't stewarded this responsibility as I should.

I grew up going to *the* sacred site of the Ku Klux Klan. No one told me that (at least that I can remember), and I never took the time to learn it. Upon graduation from school, I started traveling across the southern United States, preaching in churches and eventually serving in prominent ministry positions. Almost all the people I ministered to and the ministers I served with were White, and I never took the time to ask why. And as I'll explain more in the pages ahead, all these years I was not only ignoring racial division from the past but also contributing to its preservation in the present.

And I don't believe I'm alone.

Throughout the history of the United States and continuing today, professing Christians have perpetuated the racial divide in our country, leading *the body of Christ* to become and remain one of the most segregated institutions in American society. This must change, and living by the biblical gospel makes that change possible.

It is well past time to leave behind an American gospel that has cultivated the ownership and torture of slaves by "Christian" masters, the killing of people alongside the burning of "Christian" crosses, the lack of support for civil rights or even acknowledgment of racial disparities among "Christian" leaders, and the ongoing racial division in "Christian" churches. For centuries, the American gospel has favored and led to the prosperity of one color of people—specifically, my color of people—at the expense of another. The biblical gospel beckons us in our day to do our part to bring down walls of division and create a more beautiful picture of the church than we have experienced in our history.

WORDS LIKE STONES

Before I go further, I feel like I need to give about a million caveats and add another million disclaimers. Addressing race and ethnicity is like walking through a field of emotional, intellectual, spiritual, and extremely personal landmines. I can't know everyone who will read this book, but I do know that each of us carries our own perspective and experiences. On this subject, virtually anything I write is likely to offend someone. I realize that some of you are already offended that I'm differentiating between people based on skin color.

Offense is not my aim (unless that offense comes directly from God's Word, which, as we'll see in the next chapter, is the best kind of offense). My sincere desire is to explore how the biblical gospel radically transforms our understanding of race and ethnicity, particularly in the American church, and to share how each of us desperately needs this transformation, myself first and foremost.

I should also add that the thrust of this chapter is focused on the historic and current Black-White disparities in our country and division in the church. But as I mentioned, our church has people from more than one hundred countries, and I don't want in any way to minimize the unique challenges that Hispanic, Asian, Native American, or other sisters and brothers experience both in our country and in the church. My hope is that in using the gospel to address the clear Black-White disparities and division, we might see its power to overcome challenges for people of every ethnicity.

I know from personal experience that the minute you write or speak about race and ethnicity, someone on social media, in the pews, or in your social circles is likely to hurl labels at you like stones. And people don't usually throw stones unless they intend to do harm. I won't try to defend myself, but I will say that I grieve over the God-honoring, gospel-loving people I know who have been slanderously branded as "woke progressives" or "cultural Marxists" (i.e., likened to the author of *The Communist Manifesto*) in ways that defy logic, denigrate individuals, families, and churches, and cause real harm.

Further, let's realize that labeling tactics like this are not new and have proved to be damaging throughout our history. In 1850, at the dedication of a new and separate church building "for the religious instruction of the Negroes," prominent Christian leader and proponent of slavery James Thornwell gave a sermon "before a large assembly of intelligent and respectable citizens of Charleston" (i.e., White, professing Christian slave owners in the South).[4] He expressed the popular sentiment in the church that those people working for racial justice (specifically, freedom for slaves) were "socialists" and "communists." Consider his words, which were later published for wide distribution:

> These are the mighty questions which are shaking thrones to their centres—upheaving the masses like an earthquake, and rocking the solid pillars of this Union. The parties in this conflict are not merely abolitionists and slaveholders—they are atheists, socialists, communists, red republicans [the anti-slavery party at that time], jacobins, on the one side, and the friends of order and regulated freedom on the other. In one word, the world is the battle ground—Christianity and Atheism the combatants; and the progress of humanity the stake.[5]

In other words, this Christian leader was saying that men and women who were working for racial justice were destroying the foundations of American society and opposing the gospel at the heart of Christianity. Sound familiar?

A century later, we see similar church leaders labeling Martin Luther King, Jr., and other civil rights activists (including pastors) "communist," "socialist," and "Marxist." Morton Smith, who would later become clerk of the Presbyterian Church in America, criticized an article written by a fellow Presbyterian minister on biblical opposition to segregation, saying,

> The reason that so many see a Communist influence in the present movement is that the goal seems to be the same as that of the Marxist philosophy, namely, the levelling of all to a common uniformity. Even if the American Negro movement has not been started or backed by the Communist Party at first, it certainly plays into the hands of the Communists, especially when civil disobedience can be encouraged, and the law and order of a city, state, or nation threatened. Enough of this disorder, and the Communists or some other tyrants may be able to step into the situation and seize control of our nation.[6]

It's no surprise to hear similar labels coming from Christians and church leaders whenever the subject of racial injustice rises today. In the face of these age-old tactics, let's do what God's people have done throughout history and humbly open God's Word to see what he has to say. As we do, we will find God's guidance through the gospel more than sufficient to help us move forward into a different future.

RACE IN THE BIBLE

As a foundational matter, the Bible never defines different races according to skin tone, hair texture, or other physical traits like we do in contemporary culture. Instead, God creates all people wonderfully and equally in his image as *one human race.*

That's not to say that people aren't different according to God. The Bible teaches that though united in our humanity, we are diverse in our appearance, speech, and ethnicity. After the fall of man and the flood of the world, the Bible describes various clans dwelling in distant lands and separate nations speaking their own languages. Diverse ethnic groups with different physical attributes and distinct social patterns emerge on the human landscape, each displaying extraordinary diversity while sharing a basic and beautiful unity as image bearers of God.

This biblical reality is why we should be careful not to ignore or attempt to erase our ethnic differences. When Paul wrote in Galatians 3:28, "There is neither Jew nor Greek, there is neither slave nor free, there is no male and female, for you are all one in Christ Jesus," he wasn't saying, "There is no such thing as Jew or Greek; in Christ, your heritage is a relic of the past." He was also not saying, "There is no such thing as male or female; in Christ, your gender is no longer significant, or even existent." Instead, Paul taught that we are united in Christ and that no one is more valuable than another. No Jew is more valuable than a Greek (or vice versa), and no male is more valuable than a female (or vice versa). Indeed, it's our biblical duty to see our diversity the way God sees our diversity—as a stunning portrait of his creativity that exalts his glory as our Creator.

Certainly some will argue, "But I'm color blind. I choose not to see color in people, and that's the way we all should see." After all, Martin Luther King, Jr., envisioned a future where people "will not be judged by the color of their skin but by the content of their character."[7] Right? We might, then, conclude that it's a good thing to be color blind.

But others hear claims of color blindness and ask, "Why are you choosing to ignore part of who I am, where I've come from, and how my family's ethnicity and history have affected me, particularly in light of the fact that I've been affected in significant ways *because* of these things?" Calls for color blindness can come across as attempts to minimize a significant part of someone's heritage and makeup.

In addition, by promoting color blindness, we run the risk of diminishing the creativity of God and misunderstanding the way he sees us. Yes, God sees each of our hearts, and at the core, we're all wonderfully and equally made in his image. But biblically, it sure seems like God sees different people in different colors from different backgrounds with different histories.

Interestingly, even in heaven, we're not all going to look the same. According to Revelation 7:9–10,

> After this I looked, and behold, a great multitude that no one could number, from every nation, from all tribes and peoples and languages, standing before the throne and before the Lamb, clothed in white robes, with palm branches in their hands, and crying out with a loud voice, "Salvation belongs to our God who sits on the throne, and to the Lamb!"

For all of eternity, our diversity will be fully present, even as we experience a greater unity than we have ever known on earth.

PRONE TO PREJUDICE

The unfortunate reality is that as sinful people living in a fallen world—that's all of us, for the record—we're prone to show prejudice toward those who don't look like us or share our story. This sinful sense of pride in ourselves and others like us has led human beings to reject our common dignity as one human race and to classify races according to arbitrary characteristics like skin tone, hair texture, facial and body features, class, caste, geography, ancestry, or language. Then—consciously or not—people assign supposed values and distinct advantages (a hierarchy) to different groups based on these characteristics.

In the process of denying shared roots in the human race by devising and upholding a hierarchy of different races— which goes directly against God's Word—people commit the sin of racism: *valuing or devaluing one race (according to our classification) over or beneath another.* Expressions of racism include thoughts, feelings, words, actions, expectations, relationships, laws, policies, procedures, systems, and structures that value one race over another.

I use the phrase *expressions of racism* intentionally because we have conflicting ideas about how to use the label *racist.* People accuse (often in the most condemning tone) another of being racist, and the accused person will reply (often in a defensive or indignant tone) that he or she is not. Many people, when they hear *racist,* immediately think of the Ku Klux Klan or Jim Crow laws. Therefore, since they reject these things, they conclude, "I'm definitely not racist."

By this measure, every follower of Jesus I know would say that they are not racist. Yet immediately exempting ourselves from conversations about racism not only disrespects brothers and sisters who are hurting but also shuts down the very kind of introspection our diverse church family needs in order to heal and grow, particularly here in America. Scripture teaches that *none* of us is immune to *any* sin in our hearts, including pride, prejudice, and partiality—the sins that are at the root of expressions of racism.

Instead of arguing over who is or isn't racist, then, let's acknowledge that expressions of racism are possible in all of us. Like every other sin, these expressions could be overt or hidden. They might be consistent or passing. They might be intentional or unintentional. They might be present in an individual or a group. Regardless, the Bible—which defines ultimate reality—teaches that sinful people are prone to pride, partiality, and prejudice, which can play out in many different expressions of racism.

Expressions of racism permeate our history as human beings—in a variety of horrifying ways. Consider the Holocaust in Germany, the Armenian massacre in Turkey, the genocide in Rwanda, the Japanese slaughter of Koreans, Chinese, Indo-Chinese, Indonesians, and Filipinos, and the persecution of Rohingya Muslims in Myanmar. Each of these expressions of racism was or is rooted in the belief that one race is superior to another.

Sadly, our country isn't exempt from these horrors, which is evidenced by historical massacres of Native American peoples and the enslavement of Africans. To these horrors we should add, among other ethical failures grounded in unbiblical conceptions of race, the internment of Japanese citizens, discrimination against Irish immigrants, and the enforcement of Jim Crow laws.

As much as we would all like to distance ourselves from

the taint of racism in history, in order to make sure we don't repeat the same behavior, we need to at least acknowledge that we're not immune from the temptations that produced it. Sure, none of us is guilty of sending a Jewish person to a concentration camp because we thought Jewish people should be exterminated. Similarly, not one of us is guilty of abusing an African slave because we thought he or she was a person of lesser innate worth. But our pervasive sinfulness means that personal pride and ethnic prejudice are a present possibility in all of us. According to James 4, we're all prone to the pride before God and prejudice toward others that leads to selfishness, jealousy, fights, quarrels, and covetousness. We all face temptations to prefer people who are like us in color, culture, heritage, history, or social status. And the Bible shows that such temptations can lead us to ignore, avoid, disparage, neglect, and mistreat people who simply aren't like us. Remember the parable of the Good Samaritan in Luke 10 and the admonitions against favoritism in the church in James 2?

What may be most dangerous is that we're even inclined to use the Bible to justify our pride, partiality, and prejudice. Frightening evidence of this is found in the well-documented arguments among American Christians (including notable and otherwise well-respected church leaders) in the nineteenth century in favor of race-based chattel slavery—a practice that represented a fundamental denial of human dignity, a total abuse of God's Word, and a reprehensible distortion of God's character. We will explore this more in the next chapter, but over the centuries, Christians have used the Bible to justify human trafficking, physical torture, and denigration of people made in God's image, and we would be fools to think that we're not susceptible to abusing Scripture in similar ways.

THE DISPARITY CONTINUES

Yet even if our hearts are completely pure—which they won't be this side of heaven—we live in a country where different people continue to experience different benefits or burdens based on their skin color. Thankfully, by God's grace and the action of godly men and women, race-based chattel slavery was abolished and civil rights legislation was passed. Nevertheless, undeniable statistics demonstrate that clear racial disparities still exist.

Consider these facts pertaining specifically to Black and White Americans:

- There are approximately two unemployed Black people for every one unemployed White person, a ratio that has held constant over the last fifty years.[8]
- Black households earn about half as much as White households (and possess about 15–20 percent as much net wealth) in a wealth gap that has actually widened over recent decades.[9]
- Black babies die at more than twice the rate of White babies.[10]
- Black mothers are three to four times more likely to die in childbirth than White mothers.[11]
- Young Black males are twenty times more likely to die by gun homicides than young White males.[12]
- Black Americans are seven times more likely to be wrongfully convicted of murder than White Americans.[13]

- White Americans are substantially more likely than Black Americans to get a quality education, to have a high-paying job, and to live in a more affluent neighborhood with less crime.[14]

These facts call for more caveats. The statistics above paint a broad-brush picture, and the last thing I want to do is equate "Black" with "poor and uneducated." Similarly, I don't want to disparage or disempower my Black brothers and sisters in any way. Neither do I want to spread a blanket of guilt across all White people. Moreover, I've obviously referenced disparities only between Black and White people in general, to the exclusion of other groups like Asian Americans, Native Americans, Latin Americans, and Pacific Islanders. Lastly, I'm not even saying *why* these disparities exist, for I know we have different perspectives on the reasons behind these realities.

Yet with all the above caveats considered, these statistics lead to a staggeringly straightforward conclusion. Even if none of us wants skin color to matter in the United States, apparently it does. And it doesn't just matter in our country; it matters in the church.

Amid widespread racial disparities, the church itself stands divided over skin color, specifically white and black skin color. At the turn of the twenty-first century, at least 95 percent of White Americans attended predominantly White churches, and 90 percent of Black Americans attended predominantly Black churches[15]—a division that had existed ever since slavery and the subsequent discrimination White churches showed toward Black Christians after the Civil War. Some progress toward integrating congregations has been made in the last two decades, but as of just a couple of years ago, only 16 percent of churches were considered multiracial. And over the last couple of years, these churches (including my own church family) have experienced substantial challenges to "sustaining their multiracial composition."[16]

Are we getting this? Ever since slavery, not only has the American church failed to bridge racial divides in our country, but as we gather each week to worship God, we are in fact deepening that divide. As much as we would like to think that the church is a force for countering racial division, we have perpetuated it throughout our history, and we are still doing so today.

Surely the people of God shouldn't be comfortable with explicit racial disparities in our country and ongoing racial division in the church. Shouldn't we at least pause and seriously ask, "Why do racial disparities in our country and racial division in the church still exist?" I trust that we all hate the racism, slavery, and Jim Crow laws in our history. How, then, can we be content when so many churches, seminaries, missions organizations, and Christian conferences today look like time capsules preserving the division of the past?

CONTENT WITH DIVISION

I feel personal tension even as I ask these questions, because I have so often ignored racial disparities in my country. What's more, I regret that for so long I have proven to be quite content with racial division in the church.

I grew up in a neighborhood, attended schools, and was a member of a church where almost everyone had white skin, just like me. When I was in middle school, one of our White neighbors put their house up for sale and a Black family bought it. Word spread that housing values were going to plummet as a result, and people started moving out. I was fairly young, of course, but I never thought to question why this should be the case. Discrimination and segregation were baked into my world. (Lest we think residential segregation is a relic of the past, the degree of racial residential segregation increased from 1990 to 2019 in most U.S. metropolitan regions, and not just in the South.[17])

When I went to college, I was involved in an exclusively White fraternity and an almost exclusively White Christian campus ministry. After college, I attended an almost exclusively White seminary where almost every professor I had and nearly every author I read was White. The seminary was located within the city limits of New Orleans, where more than half the population is Black, and to say the seminary didn't reflect the diversity of the community or even the region would be a massive understatement.

During my five years in seminary, I traveled across the southeastern United States preaching in different churches almost every weekend. In the scores of churches I visited and preached in across Texas, Louisiana, Mississippi, Alabama, Georgia, Tennessee, and Florida, nearly every person attending the services was White. People with other skin colors obviously lived in each of those towns, but it never occurred to me to ask, "Why do hardly any people who aren't White come to these churches?"

After seminary, I moved to Birmingham, Alabama, a city whose name is synonymous with the civil rights movement. It acquired the nickname Bombingham in the 1950s on account of the myriad dynamite explosions used to threaten

African Americans and all those working toward racial desegregation. One of those bombings occurred on an infamous Sunday morning at a downtown church, resulting in the death of four young African American girls. I loved the city of Birmingham and the church I pastored there. Yet when I arrived, very few African Americans attended the church I pastored, and the same was true when I left. Sadly, it would take years for me to ask why that was true.

After pastoring in Birmingham, I went on to lead the International Mission Board (IMB) of the Southern Baptist Convention (SBC). The IMB is the largest missionary support organization of its kind in the world. The history of the IMB and SBC is marked with racism, as both institutions were formed in support of slavery. Each day, as I drove to my office at IMB headquarters in Richmond, Virginia, the former capital of the Confederacy, I found myself looking out over Monument Avenue, a street that at the time was lined with statues commemorating Confederate leaders. Did I ever ask why I should be okay with all of this? No. And how long did it take me to recognize that out of 4,900 missionaries serving with the IMB when I came, only twenty-seven were Black, roughly one-half of 1 percent? Entirely too long. As a result, that percentage didn't increase during my four-year tenure.

What do these stories and statistics have to say about me? Well, at least this: When I am addressing an ungodly contentment with racial division in the church, I am addressing and confessing ungodliness in my life.

LISTENING IS LEARNING

My mind, heart, and life began to change by God's grace, which is to say, not by anything I did. I simply moved to another church. I became a part of a family in metropolitan Washington, D.C., with brothers and sisters from more than a hundred countries across six continents—representing every skin color—and where worship gatherings are translated live each week into Spanish, Korean, and Mandarin Chinese.

In this church family, I learned to love sharing life and leadership with brothers and sisters who have backgrounds, experiences, and perspectives that are very different from mine. To be clear, I don't say the only way to learn God's truth as it relates to diversity is through exposure to such differences. Just because I spent time in almost all White churches and ministries, went to an almost all White seminary, and read almost all White authors doesn't mean I couldn't know God or his Word truly. But meeting people from around the world and sharing close community with them in our church has changed me. I've learned so much about God, myself, the church, and the world around me.

For example, I've learned more about the challenges that people of different colors experience in multiethnic Christian community. When we surveyed a large group of our members about challenges they experienced in our multiethnic church, 88 percent of White members said *they had not* experienced challenges. Just to make sure that number is clear, almost nine out of ten White church members said, in essence, "No problems." By contrast, 97 percent of Black members said *they had* experienced at least one challenge, and at least 50 percent of Asian, Latino, and Native American members expressed the same.

Read just a few of the comments I received from church members:

- A Black member wrote, "I feel invisible in our church. I wish others knew how being thought to be less because of your skin color affects the way you see yourself. And how hard it is that you have to fight your own mind in this [multiethnic] environment."
- A Latino member shared, "I feel like I have to put in extra effort at times to seem non-threatening and to seem more well-mannered than the next person in order to be accepted by other people."
- A Black sister who recently came to our church said, "In the past, I have felt unheard and unseen in my small groups for so long that I came to believe that I just had to change and be like all the white girls so I could be in their clique and they could ask me to hang out." She continued, saying, "I am hurt when people of a different skin color invalidate my experiences whenever I share them."
- One Asian American brother wrote, "I wonder sometimes in our church if people around me truly accept me for who I am."
- An Asian American woman who has been a church member for decades said, "Our church is representative of the prevailing divide, i.e., majority rule. Learn to live with it, work around it, or cope with it."
- Another Asian American man said, "I have just come to

accept the fact that I'm a guest in the church, and not really at home."

That last phrase—"not really at home"—is echoed in the experience of one of our pastors, Mike Kelsey, who is African American. He put it this way:

> Oftentimes, people of color are welcomed into predominantly White churches. The people are nice. We're invited to be involved. And for the most part, it's a good experience. But even when it is a good experience, there's often still this underlying feeling that I'm in the house, but it's not my home. It's like a bed-and-breakfast. I get to eat at the table. I can use all the amenities. I even get a bed and a room. But the menu is already predetermined. My pictures aren't on the wall. I can't rearrange the furniture and change the paint color. I'm a welcomed guest.

He went on to explain that simple things like the way we pray, the cultural norms we adopt, and the worship music we sing all feed into this sense of homelessness. But that's not all. He continued:

> The reality that we're welcomed guests becomes most clear and most painful when we try to raise issues of justice. Oftentimes, it feels like our presence is welcomed, but not our perspectives or priorities.

I would paint an incomplete picture if I didn't also share perspectives from church members who are White:

- One White brother shared, "I sometimes feel I'm supposed to be uncomfortable, guilty, or ashamed because I am white, and that others don't want to be in relationship with me."
- Similarly, one White sister said, "With all the things that have happened in our country over the last few years, sometimes I fear that my Black friends only pretend to like me or they pre-judge me based on the fact that I am an old white woman. It's particularly hard when I go to a friend's house and they have [the book] *White Fragility* in the living room. Do they actually see me, or some pre-conceived notion of me?"
- Interestingly, a White woman who is married to a Black man said, "Without question, unity in our church is on White terms."

I understand that these quotes are anecdotal, but to me they demonstrate the deep harm caused by the American gospel as it relates to race and ethnicity. And because we've waited so long to address these issues, forging multiethnic Christian community in America will be extremely difficult. But it will be beautiful.

While writing this chapter, I was in a meeting with leaders in our church. At one table, I saw women and men from Sri Lanka, Cameroon, South Korea, and Texas sitting together. (Yes, I know it's not a country, but many of you Texans think it is!) At another table, there were people born in China, Colombia, the United States, and Haiti. As my eyes scanned the room, I saw black, white, and brown faces. Many of these people had grown up in environments where everyone looked like them, just like I had. Still, each was willingly facing challenges and making sacrifices in order to experience uniquely countercultural, gospel-shaped family in the church.

THE GOSPEL CREATES MULTIETHNIC FAMILY

Jesus came to make multiethnic family like this possible. Ever since sin entered the world, humans have experienced not only separation from God but also division among themselves. Racism, ethnocentrism, and ethnic division have plagued history, including the era into which Jesus entered.

In the first century, a massive cultural chasm separated Jews and Gentiles. They didn't eat or associate with one another. They had different traditions, customs, and lifestyles. Jews called Gentiles dogs. But Jesus came to heal these divisions. He called twelve apostles, all of whom were Jewish, and he took those apostles to meet a Samaritan woman (i.e., an individual perceived as inferior because of both her ethnicity and her gender) at a well. While there, he called not just her but an entire community of Samaritans to follow him (John 4:1–42).

Jesus didn't stop there. Yes, he talked about new life with Jewish leaders like Nicodemus (John 3:1–21), but he also healed a Roman centurion's servant (Luke 7:1–10). He died on the cross as a ransom for all tribes and peoples (Revelation 5:9–10), and as soon as he rose from the grave, conquering sin, he commanded his disciples to go to every ethnic group in the world with the good news of his love (Matthew 28:19). After Jesus's ascension, the Holy Spirit made it even more clear that the gospel was for everyone. The Spirit fell on the apostles at Pentecost, empowering them to speak in other languages so that all nationalities and ethnicities could hear and believe (Acts 2:4). The Spirit sent Philip to share the gospel with an Ethiopian eunuch, establishing the church in North Africa (Acts 8:26–40). God sent Peter to Cornelius—a Roman centurion over the Italian Regiment—to fuel the westward spread of the gospel (Acts 10). He empowered Paul to take the good news to the Gentiles from eastern Europe to Asia Minor.

By God's good design, the early church was multiethnic.

But these Christians were not without controversy in their efforts to forge multiethnic community. When the Gentiles wanted to be baptized, included in the same church, and seated at the same tables, many Jews pushed back. The Jews were, after all, God's *chosen* people. Paul addressed this divide clearly in a letter to the Ephesians:

> Now in Christ Jesus you who once were far off have been brought near by the blood of Christ. For he himself is our peace, who has made us both one and has broken down in his flesh the dividing wall of hostility by abolishing the law of commandments expressed in ordinances, that he might create in himself one new man in place of the two, so making peace, and might reconcile us both to God in one body through the cross, thereby killing the hostility. . . . For through him we both have access in one Spirit to the Father. So then you are no longer strangers and aliens, but you are fellow citizens with the saints and members of the household of God. (2:13–19)

The biblical picture is clear. The gospel transcends the powers of the world in order to break down dividing walls and bring people from across all kinds of lines—ethnic lines included—together in the church.

So why don't we in America experience this kind of diverse community as the church, and what will it take to change that?

Entire volumes have been written and likely still need to be written addressing this question, but a critical starting point is agreeing that the question needs to be answered. After all, some say social self-sorting by ethnicity is good. We tend to like being around people who are like us, in everything from song tastes to socioeconomic levels, political leanings to personal preferences. So maybe it's better this way.

This train of thought is one reason that, for decades now, church-growth gurus have promoted what's called "the homogeneous unit principle." In essence, the thinking is that if pastors want to reach a lot of people in the church and if people like being around those who are most like them, then pastors should focus on trying to reach one type of person in their church. Other types of people will flock to another church tailored to them. The way to grow the church, the gurus say, is to appeal to a particular group's preferences, and most churches have drawn crowds by doing exactly this.

But where do we see this taught in the Bible? Where do we ever see Paul saying to Jewish people, "If you guys just stick together and keep the Gentiles out, we can reach a lot more Jews a lot faster"? Or to the Gentiles, "You start your own churches so that you don't have to put up with all these Jews"? Nowhere. Though it's quite popular and most churches have bought into it, building Christ's church by prioritizing homogeneity goes against what the Bible teaches.

In contrast to our homogeneous congregations today, the New Testament shows men and women *working hard together* across ethnic, socioeconomic, cultural, political, and preferential lines to love and care for one another like family. This means every Christian has a part to play in working hard to cultivate diverse community, to the extent possible, whether it's church leaders refusing to cater to certain types of people or church members staying committed to one another even when all our preferences aren't prioritized. The more we gladly work together like this, the more we will radiate the glory of Jesus as a people whose depth of community can be explained only by the miracle of the gospel that makes us one.

ENCOURAGEMENT FOR THE WAY FORWARD

I would be remiss if I didn't speak a specific word of encouragement to my African American sisters and brothers before this chapter closes and a specific word of exhortation to sisters and brothers who, like me, are White.

First, encouragement to my African American sisters and brothers.

I thank and praise God for his grace in your resiliency and the resiliency of your parents, grandparents, and great-grandparents who are forebearers in our faith. I'm grateful that you would choose to follow Jesus in an American church that has such a history of racial injustice. I cannot imagine being beaten (literally or metaphorically) by people who preached the Bible to me and still choosing to believe that Bible. The fact that we have strong Black churches across the

United States is a powerful testimony to the preserving grace of God and the persevering faith of African American Christians. I'm sincerely honored to be your brother in Christ. I know I still have a lot to learn, and I sincerely long to do so alongside you.

I also want to speak a specific word to my White brothers and sisters.

As you and I know, throughout our country's scarred history of slavery and racial injustice, so many White Christians and churches have been found either contributing to these evils or complacent in the face of them. I trust we all know the picture of Martin Luther King, Jr., sitting in a Birmingham jail as eight White pastors criticized his methods and called for him to be more patient. In his cell, he wrote a letter, saying,

> In the midst of blatant injustices inflicted upon the Negro, I have watched white churches stand on the sideline and merely mouth pious irrelevances and sanctimonious trivialities. In the midst of a mighty struggle to rid our nation of racial and economic injustice, I have heard so many ministers say, "these are social issues with which the gospel has no real concern."[18]

An American gospel may not have been concerned with racial injustice and division but a biblical gospel is. In his "Letter from Birmingham Jail," Dr. King went on to say,

> There was a time when the Church was very powerful. It was during that period when the early

Christians rejoiced when they were deemed worthy to suffer for what they believed. In those days the Church was not merely a thermometer that recorded the ideas and principles of a popular opinion; it was a thermostat that transformed the mores of society. . . .

But the judgment of God is upon the church as never before. If the church of today does not recapture the sacrificial spirit of the early church, it will lose its authentic ring, forfeit the loyalty of millions, and be dismissed as an irrelevant social club with no meaning for the twentieth century.[19]

Sixty years after this letter was written, we need to decide which gospel we're going to embrace and what kind of church we're going to be.

For the most part, our White forebearers did not lament their participation in racism. They certainly did not, as Dr. King wrote, "recapture the sacrificial spirit of the early church," at least in relation to the African American community. There is biblical precedent for acknowledging and grieving over this failure today. Biblical characters like Ezra and Nehemiah humbly acknowledged and lamented the sins of their predecessors, and they led God's people to turn from those sins. And time and again, God commanded his people to tear down idols and high places from previous generations so that they wouldn't be captive to sinful ways passed down to them.

This is one reason I chose to stand with and march alongside other Bible-believing, gospel-proclaiming Christians and church leaders on the streets of Washington, D.C., in June

2020. When asked to lead in prayer at the beginning of that march, I prayed that God would "forgive us for [injustice in] our history and our present" and "for the sin that so infects our heart."[20] Yet once these words were printed in a national newspaper, upset church members sent messages to me, saying, "You shouldn't confess sins you haven't committed."

While I know biblically that we are ultimately accountable before God for our own sins, I also know that the Bible shows the importance of corporate confession. Interestingly, I didn't get any pushback in the church when I corporately confessed the sin of abortion in our country from the past and present just five months prior onstage at the March for Life in Washington, even though I have never been personally involved in supporting an abortion. But even beyond this, to be clear, I meant exactly what I prayed. In light of all I have shared in this chapter, I am truly sorry for every intentional or unintentional expression of racism *in me.* I want to be free from the sin that infects my heart, and I want to repent and "recapture the sacrificial spirit of the early church."

What might this sacrificial spirit look like specifically for me and for other followers of Jesus who are White? With a history of people who look like us being the most callous toward people of other colors in our country, let's be the *quickest to confess* any hint (again, intentional or unintentional) of racial pride or prejudice that remains. In light of forebearers who erected memorials to racial injustice, let's *work hardest* to expose and erase any remaining injustice. Of all people, let's be *most concerned* by racial disparities that still exist and *most zealous* to root out any expressions of racism in and around us. With the inheritance of those before us who separated into different churches because they believed Black people were less human, let's be *most sacrificial* in our efforts to counter racial division and promote racial harmony in the church today. Indeed, let's be *most passionate* about advancing multiethnic leadership and influence in churches, conferences, seminaries, and other organizations that for far too long have been far too White.

It is past time to leave behind a picture of the church that accommodates (and reinforces) prejudices, caters to preferences, and clings to power. Let's humbly and intentionally put aside various comforts and traditions, and let's step boldly and fully into the beautiful picture God envisions for his church. Only then can we tear down the American gospel, which divides and damages, and lift up the biblical gospel, which brings equality and, ultimately, healing.

The gospel is the good news that Jesus has shed his blood on a cross for sinners so that people might be reconciled to him *and* to one another through God's grace. This revolutionary bloodline is shared by a countercultural family of multiethnic splendor called the church. The Bible describes this spiritual body and heavenly bride as a chosen race and distinct people. There is no group like it in the world: a stunning, everlasting, love-saturated, joy-infused, hope-filled, gospel-formed, Father-glorifying family made up of every color, class, tribe, and tongue.

To *all* my brothers and sisters in Christ of every color, then, let's care for and truly share life alongside one another, and let's work together for healing among so many who have been hurt by the church's approach to race in our country. In the process, let's experience the multiethnic beauty Jesus has made possible for us in our lives and in the church.

3

A PEOPLE OF COMPASSIONATE CONVICTION

The True and Kind Treasure We Hold

It's past midnight, and the only light flickering on the mud walls comes from a small candle burning in the middle of a one-room house.

In a remote valley in central Asia, a small group of my friends and our family in Christ is clustered around that candle. They exemplify what Paul wrote in Philippians about being in need (4:11–12). They're extremely poor, isolated in the middle of the rugged mountains, and disconnected from education, healthcare, and any opportunity for economic advancement. They're also persecuted. It's against the law in their country to convert to Christianity, and if even their family members or friends knew they were followers of Jesus, it could mean immediate death.

Huddled together in this house, they whisper to one another as they wait. Bashir, whose name means "bringer of good news," left the village about an hour before. Under the cover of darkness with only a faint glow from the moon, he put on his coat and journeyed two miles to a cave. See Bashir as he reaches its mouth, gets down on his hands and knees, and crawls inside, holding a small flashlight in his mouth. Imagine him making his way through crevices to a pile of rocks. Fumbling through them, he finds the treasure he is looking for.

Bashir tucks the treasure between his arm and body as he crawls backward out of the cave. Once assured that he isn't being watched, he stands and hides his treasure under his coat. Then he retraces the two miles back to the village, picking up the pace for fear he'll be caught with contraband in his possession.

The small group assembled in the house freeze in fear as they hear the rustling of feet outside the door. After tense seconds that seem like hours, the door slowly opens. Bashir steps in, quietly closes the door, sits down in the circle, and pulls out the treasure.

A Bible.

The only one in the village. The only one in the miles of mountains around them. The only copy they have of God's Word in their language.

Bashir hasn't yet learned to read, so he hands the Bible to Moska, one of the only literate women in their area. Her name means "happiness," and a smile crosses her face as she opens the book. She reads aloud in a soft voice, surrounded by ears attuned to every word.

After a couple of hours, they know that others in the village will soon be waking, so they go around the room, praying for one another. They pray for safety. But they also pray for opportunities to share what they have learned from God's Word with other people, knowing there will be great risk in doing so. When they finish, they hand the Bible back to Bashir, who proudly plays his part by hiding the treasure in his coat, stepping gently out of the house, and hurriedly returning to the cave to hide the treasure again.

When I think about Bashir, Moska, and multitudes of other sisters and brothers in Christ in settings like this, I'm reminded that only the Bible contains the truth that is worth risking life and limb to read, know, and share. It's the treasure that brings us together in the church. Not the ideals of a country or the positions of a political party. And certainly not the most popular waves of thought in an ever-changing culture.

So why are so many Christians and churches uniting around (and dividing over) opinions and preferences that aren't clearly and directly outlined in the Bible? Could it be that we have so conflated biblical ideals with American ideals that we can no longer tell the difference between the two? Or worse, are we subtly, maybe even unknowingly, twisting biblical passages to prop up what we think over and above what God has said in his Word? And in the midst of it all, are we even paying attention to the fact that emerging generations are completely disregarding his Word as they watch the way we wield it?

The good news of the gospel is that we have a Word that is truer, kinder, and far more worthy of our lives than the founding philosophy of any country, the latest position of any political party, or the newest trend in any social movement. We have a Word that holds mysterious power to bring life to the dead, healing to the damaged, and hope to the disillusioned not only in the church but also in the world. Let's come together, then, with unshakable conviction around this treasure and risk our lives sharing it with compassion for all people around us.

WHY WE CARE

After a friend invited her to attend a church small group, Sarah arrived with a mixture of curiosity and anxiety. It was the first time she had ever been in any organized Christian setting. As everyone took a seat around the living room, the leader of the group started by saying, "Let's turn to the book of John."

Reading and discussion of the Bible ensued, but Sarah was confused from the moment it started. After the meeting was over, she innocently pulled her friend to the side. "Forgive me for asking," she said, "but I'm just wondering, Who is John, and why do I care what he thinks?"

Sarah's question is a good one, and not just for those who've never attended church. Every week in the church I serve, people have the same question. Some are new to church, but some have grown up in church. I see this question often on the faces of teenagers who have come because their parents brought them. *What does this book have to do with my life?* I can name different points in my own life when I have asked the same question.

A study was conducted to gauge Americans' views of the Bible, and participants were asked whether they believed that the Bible is sufficient for meaningful living. The trend line of the answers was obvious and alarming. Among elders, those born prior to 1946, 65 percent agreed that the Bible is sufficient for meaningful living. That number decreased to 56 percent among boomers, the next classification of respondents. Among those classified as Gen Xers, the number dropped to 40 percent. Want to guess what percentage of millennials (those born between 1985 and 1998) agreed that the Bible is sufficient for meaningful living? Just 27 percent.[1]

Follow that trend line, and we start to wonder whether in a generation or two anyone in America will believe that the Bible is a sufficient and meaningful source of life.

Based on my pastoral experience, I'm going to assume most readers sometimes (or a lot of the time) wonder about these things. Part of me wants to spend the rest of this book showing how we know that the Bible is the authoritative Word of God and why it is uniquely sufficient for meaningful living, because conviction about this is critical to your life— now and forever. But other books have done this far better than I can, so I'll note a few resources below with a strong recommendation that you explore them further.[2]

Meanwhile, here's my attempt in a few short paragraphs to summarize the unparalleled wonder of God's Word.

Picture sixty-six books written by more than forty authors in three languages over the course of 1,500 years, all telling one consistent story: the gospel of Jesus Christ. No passage in the entire Bible contradicts this single narrative. Not one. Ask yourself, *How is that even possible?* If you asked forty people you know to write a book that told one overarching story about who God is, who we are, how this world was made, what's wrong in the world, and how this world can be made right, there's no chance those forty would agree. And those are all people living at the same time and likely speaking the same language. But the Bible—including books written by a farmer, shepherd, soldier, lawyer, priest, tax collector, and fisherman (just to name a few of the authors), in different languages over the course of centuries—tells one stunningly consistent story.

In contrast, and with all due respect to my Muslim friends, consider the Quran. It was composed not by forty authors in three languages over 1,500 years but by one man, Muhammad. This one man dictated his visions to his followers, and after he died, those recitations were written down. These written accounts contained discrepancies, so another man combed through the writings to determine what he believed was true, and then he burned any documents that might contradict his conclusions.

In addition, consider how reliable, accurate, and even prophetic the Bible is. We base our knowledge of certain events in world history on only a handful of historic documents. Yet we have more than five thousand complete or partial manuscripts of the Greek New Testament, more of which are found every year, and not one has ever resulted in a major revision of the Bible. This makes the Bible astoundingly reliable, just as you would expect the Word of God to be.

Moreover, other religious books—including the Quran—don't contain historical accounts like those we see in the Old and New Testaments of the Bible. Biblical accounts of history and geography have proven accurate time and time again. And that accuracy extends not only to things that *have* happened in the world but also to things that *will* happen. The Bible contains thousands of predictions that have been or are being fulfilled with uncanny exactness, including three hundred specific prophecies in the Old Testament written over hundreds of years that were fulfilled in detail in the life, death, and resurrection of Jesus. And Jesus himself affirmed the historicity, consistency, and authority of the Bible.[3]

Finally, consider how the Bible was written by eyewitnesses at great personal cost. Imagine being one of the authors of the New Testament, risking your life to write about Jesus. No one can deny what you've written about his life, death, and resurrection, because they saw the same things with their own eyes. So instead of disproving you, they threaten, imprison, and persecute you. Yet you keep writing because this truth is worth your life. As Blaise Pascal said, "I believe only the histories, whose witnesses got themselves killed."[4] And for the last two thousand years, this testimony has been passed down from generation to generation through trial and persecution, all the way to you, me, and men and women in a remote mountain village in central Asia, where it's continuing to spread today.

When we put it all together, we see that the Bible is ultimately supernatural. And not just because of its consistency, reliability, accuracy, and authority over time, but because of its ability to change lives and history when people simply read and share it. There is no book like this book.

Smoking Scripture

I think of one of our brothers in Christ named Fernando, who regularly shares the gospel on South American streets. If anyone knows the power of the Bible alone to change lives, it's him.

Carrying a New Testament in his hand, Fernando approached a man on the side of the road and struck up a conversation with him. His name was Nicholas, and he smoked a cigarette as Fernando opened the New Testament and began sharing the gospel with him. Nicholas didn't seem to be paying attention, but he looked curiously at the New Testament in Fernando's hands.

During a pause in the conversation, Nicholas said, "The paper in that book looks like it would be really good for rolling cigarettes."

Caught off guard, Fernando asked Nicholas to repeat himself.

"The paper in that book in your hand is prime smoking material."

Fernando looked down at the New Testament, then back at Nicholas, paused, and said, "Nicholas, I would like to give you this book as a gift. But I need you to promise me that before you take a page out of it to roll into a cigarette, you'll read that page. Would you promise to do that?"

Nicholas's eyes lit up. "Absolutely, I would do it. That's great paper!"

Fernando clarified, "But do I have your word that you will read a page before you tear it out?"

"You have my word."

Fernando handed him the book, wished him well, and continued down the street.

Weeks later, while walking the same street, Fernando saw Nicholas. As soon as their eyes met, Nicholas's face lit up with a smile. They shook hands as Fernando asked him, "Did you keep your word? Have you read a page in the book before tearing it out?"

"I read and smoked my way through Matthew," Nicholas eagerly explained. "Then I smoked my way through Mark and Luke. I smoked all the way to John 3, and I came to this verse that talks about how God loves the world so much that he gave his Son to die on a cross so that whoever believes in him can be forgiven of our sins and have eternal life with him. So that's what I did. I put my faith in Jesus."

This time, it was Fernando who lit up with a smile as the two brothers in Christ hugged and talked more. Their friendship continued, and the last I heard, Nicholas had become a pastor of a church on the same street where he once smoked his way through the New Testament.

Now, I'm not necessarily recommending this approach to spreading God's Word. But I am saying that God's Word alone really does have power to change lives. Not just here and now, but for all of eternity. And not just individual lives. God's Word has power to change history.

The Word Did It All

Years ago, I stood in the small room inside Wartburg Castle in Eisenach, Germany, where Martin Luther translated the New Testament into German. I knew the history that led Luther to seek refuge in the castle. After teaching people directly from the Bible, he was confronted by religious leaders in a deliberative assembly known as the Diet of Worms. There, these religious leaders threatened his life if he didn't recant his teaching of the gospel. In response, Luther famously told them, "I am bound by the Scriptures I have quoted and my conscience is captive to the Word of God. I cannot and will not recant anything."[5] As Luther traveled home from the assembly, he was taken by friends under cover of darkness to Wartburg Castle, where they would keep him hidden from the religious leaders over the next year. During that time, Luther translated the New Testament from Greek into German.

I stood in that dark castle room once home to a man who led a reformation that dramatically altered the course of history, and I couldn't help thinking about the simplicity of it all. Luther translated the Word of God into the language of ordinary people, and it totally changed their lives, their families, their country, and our history. Luther himself acknowledged this simplicity:

> I simply taught, preached, and wrote God's Word; otherwise I did nothing. And while I slept . . . or drank Wittenberg beer with my friends Philip [Melanchthon] and [Nikolaus von] Amsdorf, the Word so greatly weakened the papacy that no prince or emperor ever inflicted such losses upon it. I did nothing; the Word did everything.[6]

What a statement. How do you change lives across history? Teach the Bible, sleep, and drink beer? Well, not exactly. I'm not equating drinking beer with reforming history, but I am saying that world-changing transformation happens when God's Word is simply read, understood, believed, and spread.

THE BEST KIND OF OFFENSE

Yet even with the life-changing, history-transforming power of God's Word, we are still prone to elevate our personal ideas and positions above it, as if our thoughts are better than his truth. We shouldn't be surprised by our reckless arrogance, though. Haven't we been like this from the beginning?

Remember Adam and Eve in the Garden of Eden as a serpent whispered four little words in Eve's ear: "Did God actually say . . . ?" (Genesis 3:1). For the first time, a cluster of deadly spiritual ideas began to take hold in the world:

- Our thoughts are more trustworthy than God's truth.
- God's Word is subject to our judgment.
- We have the right, authority, and wisdom to determine what is good or evil.
- We are free to disregard God's Word when we disagree with it, or we can simply twist it to justify our disobedience to it.

In the end, Adam and Eve sinned because they believed that they knew better than God. Instead of believing that God's Word was good for them, they decided that it was offensive to them.

We share Adam and Eve's DNA. That's why it's no surprise to see a contemporary culture claiming that the Bible is offensive or to see the contemporary church elevating our ideas above God's Word. Though it may look different in each of our lives, we are all prone to exchange God's truth for what we think is right or feel is good (see Romans 1:25).

At this point, we are all both offenders and offended. We have all offended God by resisting and rebelling against his Word, and we are all offended by some (or many) parts of his Word. We naturally resist a Word that warns us against the desire for material possessions, the lust for power, and the pursuit of position. We naturally rebel against a Word that tells us to flee sexual immorality in all its forms. We are naturally prone to ignore the poor, and God's Word tells us to spend our days understanding, defending, and caring for the poor. We naturally prefer to be safe from the threats of sojourners, yet God's Word tells us to welcome them and provide for their needs. We could go on and on with all the ways God's Word offends our sinful hearts. And all these sinful tendencies are only enflamed by a culture that encourages us at every turn to live "our truth" regardless of what anyone else says—including God.

Indeed, the Bible is offensive. But offensive, I propose, in the best way possible.

What do I mean?

Our Maker loves us infinitely, and he knows what is best for us—including how we can experience life to the full. He knows it's not by following the ideologies of fallen people or the passing trends of culture. In his love for us, God has given us his Word so that we might be free from the lies of this world, which lead to death, and free to be shaped by truth, which leads to life. Shouldn't we be happily offended if something (or Someone) is leading us to abundant, eternal life?

Trust, Don't Twist

But instead of being happily offended by God's Word and reorienting our lives around it with trust in God's love, we can so subtly and almost unknowingly choose a different path— one that destroys our lives and the lives of others. Instead of trusting God's Word to form right thoughts, desires, and actions in us, we can either ignore parts of God's Word that we don't like or twist God's Word to justify sinful thoughts, desires, and actions. And maybe most dangerous of all, we can do this while we convince ourselves and others that we're following God's Word, in the end to great harm to us all.

Need proof? Consider the past and present story of Christianity in America, including the kinds of topics we're exploring in this book.

As we saw in the last chapter, the United States was built for centuries by professing Christians who twisted the Bible to say that Black people were of lesser human value—a hateful, unbiblical view that deceived generations of Christians and destroyed multitudes of lives, inflicting pain that still persists today. Such pain exists fundamentally because people ignored what God says about equality or twisted God's Word to accommodate their long-held prejudices or self-serving business models.

Similarly, as we will explore in a subsequent chapter, for centuries we have allowed pride in our nation to supplant what God says concerning all nations. Contemporary calls to make America great have resounded among Christians and illustrate how easily the church is distracted from our mandate to make Jesus great among all the peoples of the earth. As we will see, clear evidence shows that Christians and churches in our country are largely ignoring Jesus's command to make disciples of all nations, to the eternal detriment of billions of people.

Many Christians today lament about how more and more people, especially in the next generation, are denying or at least twisting what God's Word says about gender and sexuality to align with prevailing cultural trends. But should we be surprised by this, when these same people have for so long watched the church deny or twist what God's Word says about issues of race and justice among the nations? The reality we all need to face is clear: All of us are prone to defy God's Word even as we convince ourselves that we're following it.

We could go on with example after example to illustrate how desperately we need to open our Bibles together with humility, continually aware of our tendency to pick and choose the parts of God's Word that align with our opinions and preferences or to twist God's Word to fit our desires and lifestyles. And when God's Word offends our thoughts on money, materialism, prosperity, poverty, unity, refugees, racism, gender, sexuality, marriage, mission, or any other issue in our lives and our country—and it will—we need to repent of every way we don't align with what God says, then resolve to reorient our lives around the truth.

Memorize the Book

Obviously, if we're going to orient our entire lives around God's Word, we need to know what God says. How well, then, do we actually know the Bible? I think of an article I read recently about a twelve-year-old Muslim boy in Charlotte who had spent four years memorizing the entire Quran. Another article described how nine-year-old Muslims in Philadelphia have eagerly started the same process. While these children speak English, they are memorizing the Quran in Arabic since that's the original language in which it was written. All of this, of course, is with the support of their parents and faith community.

Can you imagine a church's children's ministry teaching children to memorize the entire New Testament in Greek? Then moving on to the Old Testament in Hebrew? Or maybe just starting with memorizing one book of the Bible in English? If these parents and their mosques are that committed to helping children memorize the words of a false god and if these children are that committed to actually doing it, then what might that say about our commitment as people who claim to have the words of the one true God?

If we're going to elevate God's truth above our thoughts and pass this treasure on to the next generation, then we need to get serious about hiding this truth in our hearts. At some point, we have to stop endlessly scrolling through our phones and watching our screens, filling our minds with messages from this world, and start spending our time saturating our minds with God's Word.

A WORD FOR HEALING

Then, as we learn God's Word, let's use it to lead others to eternal life. Let's share God's Word, not as a weapon to wound enemies in cultural battles but as a balm to heal and restore friends, neighbors, and strangers with the compassion of Jesus.

Not long ago, as our church walked through 1 Corinthians and came to chapters 6 and 7 (passages that contain teaching on sexuality and marriage), I read a letter from a follower of Jesus who had expressed nervousness about this subject because he experiences same-sex attraction. He wrote,

This is not a letter I want to write but I feel compelled given the upcoming message on homosexuality. There's this strange sense of foreboding, not because of fear of what you will say but for fear of being further ostracized from the church. I believe the Bible is God's Holy Word and I know what it teaches about homosexuality. I have prayed for over 20 years that this thorn would be taken from me but here I sit, still struggling and not knowing where to turn. Not giving in to a lifestyle that would displease God is in some ways the easy part. What I don't know and have never heard taught is this: how am I to relate to the church and how should the church relate to me? Will there ever be a place for people like me in a Christian community? I have lost so many friends, generally Christians, who have pulled away after the growing realization that I'm probably something they're not. I am trying to live a life of obedience, but in so doing it's even more devastating to have people who bear the name of Christ retreat from me in friendship. I guess here's my ask: as a Christian community, please don't make me choose between a life of isolation and a life that dishonors God. Figure out a way to let me in, to hold me accountable, to let me belong, to serve God, to serve the church. And if you know someone like me, don't freeze him or her out. You're our lifeline. We could sure use one . . .

Signed,

Outside Looking In

I grieved when I read those words. I saw this person: a brother in Christ who felt unseen and misunderstood in the family of Christ. He was hurt and pushed away, not because of what God's Word says about his life but because of how God's Word has been handled in the church.

Sadly, this person is not alone. I have had two conversations in just the last week with women who were sexually abused by men who were teaching them the Bible. In a horrifyingly dangerous way, the promise of safety in God's Word was exploited to harm God's children. Such evil is a dreadful distortion and absolute defiance of the Bible and its Author.

Yet none of us is immune to using the Bible to cause harm. Can I say that one more time just to make sure it soaks in? You and I are not immune to using the Bible to hurt others.

Martin Luther, the hero of the reformation I shared about earlier, once called Jews "base, whoring people" whose synagogues, schools, and homes should be destroyed.[7] What's worse, he used the Bible to back up his anti-Semitism.

Similarly, I think about Frederick Douglass's autobiography, in which he described how the more religious (i.e., "Christian") a slaveowner was, the more brutal was his or her treatment of slaves. He wrote,

In August, 1832, my master attended a [church] camp-meeting . . . and there experienced religion. I indulged a faint hope that his conversion would lead him to emancipate his slaves, and that, if he did not do this, it would, at any rate, make him more kind and humane. I was disappointed in both these respects. It neither made him to be humane to his slaves, nor to emancipate them. If it had any effect on his character, it made him more cruel and hateful in all his ways; for I believe him to have been a much worse man after his conversion than before. Prior to his conversion, he relied upon his own depravity to shield and sustain him in his savage barbarity; but after his conversion, he found religious sanction and support for his slave-holding cruelty. He made the greatest pretensions to piety. His house was the house of prayer. He prayed morning, noon, and night. . . . His activity in revivals was great, and he proved himself an instrument in the hands of the church in converting many souls. His house was the preacher's home. They used to take great pleasure in coming there to put up; for while he starved us, he stuffed them.[8]

As an example of the religious sanction his master found for his cruel actions, Douglass wrote,

I have seen him tie up a lame young woman, and whip her with a heavy cowskin upon her naked shoulders, causing the warm red blood to drip; and, in justification of the bloody deed, he would quote this passage of Scripture—"He that knoweth his master's will, and doeth it not, shall be beaten with many stripes."[9]

God, help us to learn and remember what history teaches us: The Bible can be perversely misapplied by even the sincerest of believers. The Word of Life can be used to injure, oppress, and exploit. And that is not who our God is or what he wants for us or others.

THE CALL TO KINDNESS AND HONOR

It's not enough to simply read these stories. We need to pause and ask ourselves how we might be wielding God's Word in ways that cloud God's love in the eyes of the world around us. Let's honestly examine ourselves as people who claim to promote the Word of the God who so loved the world that he gave his only Son to die for them (John 3:16). Let's humbly ask and answer questions like these:

- Do more liberal members of school boards in our country think, *Christians are the most loving people in our community*?
- What about abortion rights activists? Do they think, *Christians have shown such kindness and compassion toward me*?
- Do our self-professing lesbian, gay, bisexual, transgender, intersex, queer and questioning, asexual, and ally neighbors know us personally as friends who listen closely to them and care deeply for them?
- What about the members of the opposing political party? Do they think, *That person may disagree strongly with me, but I always feel honored and cared for by them*?
- What about our neighbors of other ethnicities? Do they see us intentionally tearing down walls of division and creating spaces where we learn about and appreciate our cultural differences?

- What about our Muslim neighbors? Would women wearing hijabs feel welcome in our churches? Do Muslims in our communities think, *That church believes differently than we do, but they are the most loving people to us, never afraid of us, and always hospitable to us?* Could the same be said about us by Muslims around the world?

As I examine my own life and ask these questions in the church I serve, I think about the temptation we all face to brandish God's Word like it's a weapon in our cultural battles. And we can point to scriptures that seem to support us. After all, it's right (according to God's Word) to care about what is taught in schools, to defend the unborn, to promote biblical sexuality, to hold positions of all kinds (including political ones) informed by Scripture, and to oppose the false teachings of Islam and other religions. Yet God's Word also calls us to show kindness, compassion, friendship, honor, love, and hospitality to all people, especially those who are different from us. If we show kindness, compassion, friendship, honor, love, and hospitality only to those who are like us, then what does that say about us? Isn't that basically just love for ourselves disguised as love for others?

Lest I be accused of glossing over scriptures, yes, Ephesians 6:17 describes the Word of God as the sword of the Spirit. Yet right before that, Paul reminds us that we are not fighting battles against *other people* (verse 12). We are *for* people, not *against* them, which according to Ephesians 6:19 means we are continually proclaiming the good news of God's love to them. We do so as we fight battles against spiritual forces of evil in this world (our real enemies), including the ever-present temptation in our own lives to doubt, distrust, manipulate, or minimize God's Word.

CONVICTION AND COMPASSION

This is the battle that Bashir, Moska, and so many others around the world are fighting in places where even having a Bible could cost them their lives. Whenever I visit sisters and brothers in settings like this, I am always struck by two particular qualities in them.

One, they possess evident *conviction* about the value of God's Word. I speak regularly at conferences for adults or students in my country, and I usually give a thirty- to sixty-minute talk once or twice, surrounded by all sorts of free time and other activities. But when I meet with Christians in persecuted countries, they come together at the risk of their lives to study God's Word for twelve hours a day. Moreover, I see their passion to pass on their knowledge of God to the next generation. I think of gathering on multiple occasions with students from their churches for secret retreats—also at the risk of their lives—and training these teenagers from early morning to the middle of the night to spread God's Word not just in their country but in surrounding countries. These sisters and brothers, including teenagers, love God's Word like nothing else in the world.

That leads to the second quality: They possess remarkable *compassion* for people who need God's Word. Neither the adults nor the teenagers above are studying the Bible for themselves, only to stay silent about it in the world. To be sure, that would be a lot easier for them. Christians don't get persecuted in these countries if they keep God's Word to themselves. They get persecuted when they share God's Word with others. But these adults and teenagers deeply love others who don't know Jesus. During my times with them, I have seen them fall on their faces, weep, and pray for people who don't know the gospel in their villages, in their cities, and in neighboring countries. Keep in mind that in many cases the people for whom these Christians are praying are the same people who are persecuting them. Yet these Christians know that the Bible teaches that these people will go to eternal condemnation if they don't hear and believe the gospel, and these Christians want to do everything they can to love them and lead them to Jesus. That's why they rise to their feet and leave these secret gatherings to spread God's Word with literally death-defying compassion.

Two qualities: conviction and compassion. They're clear in Bashir, Moska, and so many others in the church around the world. What about us? Though we don't have to gather in secret or hike to a cave to retrieve God's Word, let's revere it for the treasure that it is. With steadfast conviction and humble confidence in its supernatural value, let's not hold back from meditating on and memorizing it day and night when we're alone and studying it unashamedly for hours at a time when we're together. And as we do this, for God's sake, others' sake, and our own sake, let's guard against our every tendency to twist it, weaponize it, add to it, take away from it, or elevate our thoughts above it. Then let's rise to our feet and faithfully pass this treasure along to others, from coming generations to all nations, with the compassion of Christ himself.

4

OVERFLOWING JUSTICE

Doing What God Requires

"Do you miss your old life?"

This is the question I asked Naomi, a member of our church and an immigrant who'd experienced nothing short of a radical transformation in her life. She and her husband, Zelalem (we call him Dr. Zee), are from Ethiopia, and they'd come to the United States to pursue the American dream. Dr. Zee was extremely successful, and they lived in a beautiful house, owned the nicest things, and took the most luxurious vacations. And don't misunderstand—they were good and generous people. But they were content with a comfortable, cultural version of Christianity until one of their vacations turned everything in their family—and, more importantly, their faith—upside down.

Naomi and Dr. Zee were on a trip back to their home

country, and Naomi took a day away from her relaxation at the hotel to visit a family member who ran an orphanage. Ethiopia's orphan crisis is well documented. The country is home to millions of vulnerable children, many of whom have been orphaned by the HIV/AIDS epidemic, and many of whom live on the streets of cities like the capital, Addis Ababa. But like most Americans, Naomi was unaware of this crisis until she visited that orphanage.

I've written before that orphans are easy to ignore until you know their names or hold them in your arms, and that proved true for Naomi. Not only did she come face-to-face with these children, but she also encountered the unhealthy environments in which they lived. In fact, she learned that in one orphanage an average of four children were dying every week.

Naomi's heart was broken by the needs of these orphans, and when she returned home, she was determined to do something about it. She began to spread the word in our church and invited people closest to her to take action with her, and that's when things began to change. We began to change. Hundreds of members from our church began traveling to Ethiopia to care for orphans there. We linked arms with hundreds of Ethiopia's national churches who began implementing orphan care initiatives.

The result?

Thousands of orphans are now receiving physical nourishment on a daily basis and spiritual nourishment through discipleship programs.[1] Naomi and Dr. Zee have adopted two Ethiopian boys into their family, and some of the highest-ranking Ethiopian government officials have followed their lead. We've met with the president of Ethiopia to explore ways to expand orphan care around the country. And in that orphanage where four children were dying every week, children are now living and thriving.

I've traveled to Ethiopia with Naomi and Dr. Zee on multiple occasions. On one of those visits, I stood in a sea of hundreds of street children on a muddy hillside. Surrounded by five- to fifteen-year-old girls and boys with dirt-stained bodies barely clothed in rags, I watched them share the meager bags of food scraps they had collected in the streets that day. Younger kids smiled as teenagers offered them each a handful of lentils and injera they had scoured from the trash at restaurants and homes. Naomi walked into the center of that group of children, and they all turned to her. She commanded their attention with her kindness, and she shared different ways they could get help.

That night, I gathered the hundred or so of our church members who were serving on this trip. I stood before them with Naomi and asked her to share how God was working in, through, and around her in ways that exceeded her imagination. When she was finished sharing, I asked, "Naomi, do you miss all the vacations you used to go on and the stuff you used to get? Do you miss your old life?"

Naomi laughed. "No way, Pastor!" she said. "*This* is life!"

Naomi is right, and the Bible backs her up. God has told us how we can experience the good life. The prophet Micah wrote,

> He has told you, O man, what is good;
>   and what does the LORD require of you
> but to do justice, and to love kindness,
>   and to walk humbly with your God? (6:8)

That's exactly what Naomi is doing: justice. Specifically, she's obeying God's command to "bring justice to the fatherless" (Isaiah 1:17). She's doing justice in ways that reflect the kindness and humility of Jesus.

Sadly, however, we live in a time when followers of Jesus seem more interested in debating justice than doing it. Even as we are surrounded by countless people who are orphaned, widowed, impoverished, oppressed, enslaved, displaced, and abused, in our country and beyond our country, we expend so much energy on social media criticizing and shouting at one another about justice—feeling somehow that *this* is doing justice.

But if more of us made a calculated decision to follow in Naomi and Dr. Zee's footsteps and engage in holistic, biblical, gospel-proclaiming, Jesus-exalting justice—if we started holding more orphans in our arms, helping more widows in our communities, providing for more of the poor in our cities, serving more refugees in our country, hosting more immigrants in our homes, rescuing more slaves from traffickers, visiting more people in prison, caring for more victims of abuse, or coming alongside more moms and dads facing unwanted pregnancies—we would discover that doing biblical justice goes far beyond posting on social media, making an argument in the political arena, or even voting in an election. We would understand at long last that loving kindness is a fundamental part of what it means to follow Jesus in our everyday lives. And in the end, we would realize that doing justice and loving kindness is how we actually experience the good life in Jesus.

SILENCE IS NOT AN OPTION

Maybe you've heard this all-too-common objection: "But we shouldn't be talking about justice—we should just be preaching the gospel." Maybe you've even said it. I hear variations of this sentiment every time I say anything about racial justice, orphan care, immigration and refugees, or other justice-related topics. And it's not just me. Other pastors have similar experiences.

For many years, I allowed this sort of thinking to shape my preaching. I have written, for example, about how for far too long I was shamefully silent and passive concerning the issue of abortion. I viewed abortion as a political issue, not a biblical issue. In other words, I was "just preaching the gospel" while saying nothing on behalf of millions of children dying each year in their mothers' wombs.

When I repented of my silence and began preaching what God's Word says about the lives he is fashioning in the womb, I knew God was calling me not just to *speak* about his care for children but to *do* something about it. By God's grace, Heather and I were able to adopt, and we've made adoption and foster care a significant focus in our church family. Today our family and church partner with adoption and foster care agencies, pregnancy care centers, and other organizations working in all kinds of ways on behalf of not only the unborn but also the moms and dads who might see abortion as their best option (for a variety of reasons that we must also address).

You know what's interesting, though? Rarely (if ever) has someone in the church pushed back against my teaching on abortion. I don't hear, "Just keep your head down, teach the Bible, and stop talking about abortion." Similarly, I never hear people in the church make this argument when I speak about gender, sexuality, marriage, or religious liberty for Christians. Yet when I speak about religious liberty for Muslims, the evil of racism, caring for refugees, stopping oppression, or defending the poor, I'm likely to hear, "Just keep your head down and preach the gospel."

But why? Why are we so conveniently selective about which issues of justice are okay to speak about from the Bible in the church and which are not?

I want to assume the best about those who have these concerns, and I agree that, throughout church history, many calls for justice have indeed betrayed the gospel. Christians and church leaders have at various times and in significant ways exchanged the biblical gospel for a gospel that is satisfied to feed the poor or give shelter to the immigrant without sharing the greatest gift of all—salvation through Jesus. I want nothing to do with that kind of false gospel.

But just because some have diluted or disregarded the gospel of Jesus in calls for justice doesn't mean we should remain passive in a world full of poverty, oppression, abortion, orphans, widows, slaves, refugees, and racism. Jesus didn't. He did justice and loved kindness, and if we call ourselves his followers, we must do the same. God *requires* this of us.

Through the prophet Isaiah, God spoke sternly to his people about their pious dismissal of injustice in their midst:

Bring no more vain offerings;
    incense is an abomination to me.
New moon and Sabbath and the calling of
      convocations—
    I cannot endure iniquity and solemn assembly.

Your new moons and your appointed feasts
    my soul hates;
they have become a burden to me;
    I am weary of bearing them.
When you spread out your hands,
    I will hide my eyes from you;
even though you make many prayers,
    I will not listen;
    your hands are full of blood.
Wash yourselves; make yourselves clean;
    remove the evil of your deeds from before my eyes;
cease to do evil,
    learn to do good;
seek justice,
    correct oppression;
bring justice to the fatherless,
    plead the widow's cause. (1:13–17)

God hates it when his people say prayers, bring offerings, and attend worship services while ignoring injustice and oppression around them.

God used similar language in Amos 5 when he told his people not only what he hates but also what they should hate:

Hate evil, and love good,
    and establish justice in the gate. . . .
"I hate, I despise your feasts,
    and I take no delight in your solemn assemblies.
Even though you offer me your burnt offerings and grain
      offerings,

I will not accept them;
and the peace offerings of your fattened animals,
I will not look upon them.
Take away from me the noise of your songs;
to the melody of your harps I will not listen.
But let justice roll down like waters,
and righteousness like an ever-flowing stream."
(verses 15, 21–24)

The Bible is clear. God isn't honored by our voices when they are quick to sing songs of praise but slow to speak out against injustice. He isn't honored by our hands when they are quick to rise during worship but slow to work against wrongdoing and inequity in our communities. People who truly worship the God above them will love doing good for people in need around them.

And according to Amos, God doesn't merely require us to do acts of justice here or there in order to check a box on our to-do list. God requires us to do a lot of justice all the time, to let our works of justice overflow like a pitcher under an ever-flowing faucet. With hundreds of references in the Bible to the poor, more than a hundred references to the oppressed, more than a hundred references to orphans, widows, and so-journers, and countless references to God's concern for all people regardless of the color of their skin, we can't ignore God's heart for justice and we don't need to be cautious about doing it. By the Spirit of Jesus in us, we need to go overboard in this work.

If we don't, how much will God actually be pleased by our amped-up worship services?

WHO DEFINES JUSTICE?

But what is justice? We see this word in a variety of places, and we're all being discipled in what it means. The question is, Are we being discipled by the world or by God's Word?

Politicians, journalists, and celebrities—to name a few— all do their best to shape how we define words like *justice* and *oppression*. Further complicating matters, pithy posts on social media and sound bites from popular podcasts influence our thinking and beliefs. And it's easy to forget that invisible marketing algorithms are at work behind the scenes, dictating what we hear and see in the first place. We're virtually surrounded by opinions we like and agree with—but that obviously doesn't mean these thoughts align with God's Word.

That's why a group of approximately one thousand people in our church, at the height of the pandemic and racial and political tensions in our country, fasted, prayed, and opened our Bibles together. We wanted to know how God defined justice, and we observed that biblical justice is *that which is right for people as exemplified in the character of God and expressed in the Word of God.*

Interestingly, the Hebrew and Greek words in the Bible that we translate as "justice" and "righteousness" are often interchangeable. But sometimes we see "justice" standing alone, and in that context, it usually refers to the way we relate to other people, specifically in legal, commercial, or social matters. Consider these examples:

> You shall not pervert justice. You shall not show partiality, and you shall not accept a bribe. (Deuteronomy 16:19)

> Do justice and righteousness, and deliver from the
> hand of the oppressor him who has been robbed.
> And do no wrong or violence to the resident alien,
> the fatherless, and the widow. (Jeremiah 22:3)

God is particularly concerned about justice on behalf of the poor and oppressed, evident in examples like these from Psalms:

> The LORD works righteousness
>   and justice for all who are oppressed. (103:6)

> I know that the LORD will maintain the cause of the
>   afflicted,
>   and will execute justice for the needy. (140:12)

God is the rock whose "work is perfect" and whose "ways are justice" (Deuteronomy 32:4), and he is "the LORD who practices steadfast love, justice, and righteousness in the earth" (Jeremiah 9:24). This means that when we do justice and show mercy toward people, particularly the poor and oppressed, we're reflecting the very nature of God.

It's significant to emphasize how justice is doing not only that which reflects God's character but also that which is *right* according to God's Word. We've all noticed how the word *right* gets applied in ways that are, well, *not* right. Courts in the United States say it's right for you to marry someone of the same gender, but God's Word says otherwise. Some states in our country say it's right to take the life of an unborn child in the womb, but God's Word does not.

Many of us—even in the American church—act like it's right to be wealthy, comfortable, and secure while we functionally ignore or even push down the poor and broken. But as we've seen in Isaiah and Amos, this isn't right before God. In fact, the Bible calls it sin—rebellion against what God says is right.

INJUSTICE AND THE GOSPEL SOLUTION

Injustice, then, is that which is *not* right for people as exemplified in God's character and expressed in God's Word. Examples of injustice abound among men and women made in God's image. We lie, murder, oppress, abuse, cheat, bribe, steal, slander, and enslave. We take advantage of others to benefit ourselves. We hoard our resources. We assert ourselves as superior to others. We plunder and ignore the poor, the weak, the widow, the orphan, and the sojourner. This is the story of men and women in the Bible. And it's our story too. We're all prone to do injustice.

Injustice isn't limited to our individual actions or to our relationships either. It permeates the institutions, laws, and policies that sinful people create and maintain. Injustice isn't limited to a specific cultural moment in a particular country, and it isn't confined to one issue. Injustice manifests itself in countless ways across every country that exists. Including the United States.

So how does the true gospel help us in a world, and a country, filled with injustice?

At the center of God's Word, the good news of Jesus shines as our only hope for ultimate justice. Jesus is the Son of God who perfectly reveals the character of God, perfectly fulfills the Word of God, and perfectly demonstrates the justice of God.

Jesus is the personification of justice. Not only did he bring a taste of justice to the widows, the poor, and the sick while he was on earth; he also came to bring ultimate justice by enduring the judgment that people in all nations deserve. Jesus Christ, the Righteous One, paid the price for the sins of the world so that anyone anywhere who trusts in him can be justified before God.

Such justification before God inevitably leads to doing justice with God through the power of Jesus at work in us. According to the book of James, this is what faith in Jesus is all about:

> What good is it, my brothers, if someone says he has faith but does not have works? Can that faith save him? If a brother or sister is poorly clothed and lacking in daily food, and one of you says to them, "Go in peace, be warmed and filled," without giving them the things needed for the body, what good is that? So also faith by itself, if it does not have works, is dead.
>
> But someone will say, "You have faith and I have works." Show me your faith apart from your works, and I will show you my faith by my works. (2:14–18)

In other words, faith without justice is a farce. If we don't do justice, we don't actually know Jesus.

The starting point for doing justice, then, is realizing we need Jesus not only to save us from the injustice in our hearts but also to teach and enable us to do justice in our lives. By the power of the gospel, we need Jesus to produce in us justice and kindness that is more comprehensive, more costly, and more uncomfortable than we could ever manufacture ourselves. A longing for the good of others, particularly the poor and oppressed, that won't let us sit back and do little to nothing. A love that will move us beyond a sense of religious duty to authentic delight in doing that which is right for others in need.

PAINTING A PICTURE

I could easily write a whole book about all the practical ways we can do justice and display kindness in the world around us. For now, though, I would just encourage you to consider a few practical ways to do justice and to meditate on some of the Scriptures below.

- Proclaim the gospel here and among all nations. As we'll see in the next chapter, it is *not right* that billions of people still haven't heard the good news about Jesus, and God commands us to change this reality (Matthew 28:18–20; Acts 1:8; Romans 15:14–21).
- Love your spouse, children, and parents in your home, and help people who are being abused or oppressed in their homes (Ephesians 5:22–6:4).[2]
- Work with compassion and concern for vulnerable individuals and groups, including orphans, widows, so-

journers, individuals and families with special needs, and single parents (Exodus 22:21; Psalm 82:3–4; Isaiah 1; Jeremiah 22:13–16; Ezekiel 22:29–31; James 1:27).

- Correct oppression, and protect people from sexual abuse, prosecute sexual abusers, and create systems and structures for appropriate accountability and prevention of sexual abuse (Exodus 3:9; Deuteronomy 26:7; 2 Kings 13:4; Psalm 9:9; 103:6; Ezekiel 45:9).
- Steward advantages you have for the sake of the disadvantaged around you. Americans have advantages that Somalis don't have, and some Americans have advantages that other Americans don't have, so justice and mercy ask, "What advantages do I have that I can use to help the disadvantaged?" (Matthew 25:14–46; Luke 12:41–48; 2 Corinthians 8:1–9; 9:6–15).[3]
- Understand the needs and defend the rights of the poor and oppressed (Proverbs 29:7; 31:8–9; Isaiah 1:17).
- Be honest in financial dealings (don't take bribes or extort money), and penalize people for dishonest financial dealings (Proverbs 17:23).
- Speak honestly to and kindly about others, even (or especially) those with whom you disagree. Injustice includes slander, which ironically happens quite frequently in discussions about justice in the church (Proverbs 10:11; Ephesians 4:29–32).
- Use any authority you have to serve and build up others (Mark 10:41–45; Philippians 2:5–11).
- Honor and pray for all people, particularly your government leaders (1 Timothy 2:1–6; 1 Peter 2:17).
- Subject yourself to the government and pay taxes. April 15 in the United States, according to the book of Ro-

mans, is a day to worship God by paying taxes to governmental authorities (13:1–7).

- Do hard, honest work. In the early church, Christians in Thessalonica were quitting their jobs because they said Jesus was coming back soon. Paul knew this was a disruption to the local economy and to Christians' ability to provide for themselves and those in need. So he wrote them a letter that included this simple message: Get a job (2 Thessalonians 3:6–15; see also Colossians 3:23–24).
- Promote justice in institutions, laws, and policies that affect other people. This means promoting just laws for all people to live and work by and the impartial execution of those laws, as well as working so that all people have access to opportunities. This process includes honestly acknowledging that not all people are starting from the same place (Leviticus 19:15–18, 35–36; Deuteronomy 16:19–20; Psalm 72:4; Proverbs 13:23; 20:23).
- Work so that people who have been wronged are rightly restored (Exodus 21:33–22:15, 25–27; Numbers 5:5–10; Luke 19:1–10).[4]
- Love your enemies and leave vengeance to God (Matthew 5:43–48; Romans 12:19–21).

The list above is not intended to be exhaustive, and it's certainly not a list of boxes for us to check. But taken together, it paints a picture of justice and kindness flowing from the life that has been transformed by the love of Jesus.

Marisa

When I think about what it looks like to do justice, so many names come to mind. One is Marisa.

Marisa has cerebral palsy and spends her days in a wheel-chair. When she first came through the doors of our church, she was welcomed into our family as people cared for her special needs and ultimately introduced her to the One who could meet her deepest need. I'll never forget the day when Marisa was baptized. As a church member held her above the water, she shared with our church family,

> At one point in my life, I hated going to church because I was usually shoved into a corner. This changed when I came to this church. I was thir-teen years old, and I wanted to go to camp with the other kids my age. Someone offered to go with me and help me with all my physical needs. That camp was life-changing for me. It was the first time I came into a church and felt accepted—like they actually wanted me there, praying and wor-shipping and having fun with them. During that camp, I gave my life to Jesus. That didn't mean life got easier. Being in a wheelchair already alien-ated me from my classmates at school, and when I tried to share about Jesus with them, that alien-ated me even more. I really didn't have friends at school, but I had a family here at church who loved me.

In whatever worship gathering she is a part of, Marisa wheels her chair to the front row, where she sings loudly and listens attentively to God's Word. If you ever listen to the audio of sermons when Marisa is present, you'll inevitably hear loud amens coming from a chair near the front, and now you'll know who it is.

We follow Jesus by doing justice for and showing kindness to individuals and families with special needs.

Habib

When I consider doing justice, I also think about a sojourner named Habib. In Scripture, the word *sojourner* can be translated as "immigrant," and it's similar to *refugee*. It describes people who are separated from their families and land, often finding themselves in precarious positions and needing help from the people among whom they now live. Over recent years, we have witnessed a refugee crisis like never before in history, with nearly ninety million people forced from their homes.[5] Habib is one of these.

Most Americans pay little attention to the refugee crisis, and what attention we give to it is usually through the lens of political punditry and partisan debates over what is best for us. It's a sure sign of American self-centeredness when we take the suffering of millions of people and turn it into an issue about ourselves—our rights, our jobs, or our way of life. And the American church is no different. Research shows that specifically White evangelical Protestants are among the most resistant to the reception of refugees in our country.[6]

Thankfully, though, Habib's story is different. He has been a refugee since birth. His parents fled with him from violence in Israel and went to Iraq. He met his wife there, and when she was eight months pregnant, they were forced by militants to flee to Jordan, where they hid in a mosque and had their baby. Eventually they ended up in a refugee camp in a harsh desert on the Iraq-Syria border where they lived for six years before coming to the United States. They were welcomed by a church group who met them at the airport and began the process of helping Habib and his wife find work and their kids find schools. But they didn't just help Habib find work and educational opportunities for his kids; they shared the love of Christ with him. By God's grace, through the justice done by followers of Jesus, this family now knows the gospel.

We follow Jesus by doing justice for and showing kindness to sojourners.

Randy and Courtney

God saved Randy and Courtney from cultural Christianity, which had robbed them of true life in Christ for the first thirty-plus years of their lives. I was preaching through the book of Ruth when Courtney, deep in bondage to hidden sin, heard God's voice almost audibly say: "I love you." When she surrendered to his love, having fully turned from herself to trust in Jesus, he filled her and Randy with supernatural compassion. Before long, that compassion expressed itself in a desire to care for the homebound, particularly widows. Randy is an electrician by trade, and Courtney is a nurse practitioner, so they started looking for opportunities to do exactly what James 1:27 says: "to visit . . . widows in their affliction."

To be clear, when the Bible describes visiting widows, it means more than occasionally saying hello. The same word for "visit" in James 1:27 is used to describe how God himself visits his people to help, restore, strengthen, and encourage them. Visiting widows means seeking them out with a deep concern for their well-being and a clear commitment to care for their needs. It means using everything at our disposal to love them.

That's exactly what Randy and Courtney did and what they mobilized others to do with them. They now spend their weekends—and many days during the week—doing fairly unglamorous deeds in widows' homes. Rewiring electricity. Fixing plumbing. Building wheelchair ramps. Cleaning bathrooms. Changing diapers. Delivering medicine. They stay with many of these widows to their last breath.

I've heard from some of the people Randy and Courtney have helped, and I'd love for you to hear from them too:

- "Randy and Courtney are my friends. They are my family. I believe that God sent them to me to encourage me and to help me. Sometimes I ask God if they are even real. It's like God has sent me some angels to take care of me. They pray with me; they help me with my house; they always come and check on me; they bring me food and groceries; they read the Bible with me. I know that they care. Sometimes I just feel like I want to cry because I am so thankful to God for sending them."
- "When I see Jesus, I'm going to tell him everything Randy and Courtney did to help me and serve me and take care of me."
- "I spent over twenty years without a friend. Then Randy and Courtney became my friends. They have given their lives to show mercy to people like me. To me, that is the very picture of who Jesus is."

The woman who said the words above was elderly and disabled and recently went to be with the Lord. She died holding her friend Courtney's hand.

We follow Jesus by doing justice for and showing kindness to widows.

Patricia

Finally, let me introduce you to Patricia and her children. A couple of church members and I visited Patricia in what, from the outside, seemed to be a modest but nice four-bedroom home in a relatively good neighborhood. Recognizing us from the church, Patricia welcomed us into her house with a smile and a child about a year old in her arms. After we left some groceries we'd brought in the kitchen, she invited us to have a seat on the meager furniture in the living room. We did, and she shared her story.

In broken English, Patricia said she'd recently fled from El Salvador after her husband was killed by drug traffickers. Convinced it was no longer safe for her to stay in her country, her parents sacrificed all the money they had so she and her children could move to the United States. She came into the country with her two sons, one of whom was the child she was holding. The other, she said, was upstairs in his room because he had a severe physical handicap that made it hard for him to even walk, much less come downstairs.

It was a difficult story, but that wasn't all. Up to that point in the conversation, I assumed Patricia and her boys were the only ones living in this house. But then she explained that she was renting a single room in the house. Three other families rented the other rooms. None of them could afford a house or an apartment, because all of them struggled to make ends meet through day labor. So they shared living quarters with strangers, hoping their housemates were safe. What's more, she shared how she hoped her landlord was decent. She'd heard stories of women who were required to provide "services" for property owners when they couldn't make rent.

Having visited Patricia's shared home, I can't deny that a child who is born into my home—with a mom and a dad, a stable income, access via insurance to the best medicine in the world, and access to high-quality education—begins life with very different advantages from Patricia's children. Consequently, I can't help but ask, Doesn't doing justice and loving kindness in some way mean working to provide fair opportunities for Patricia's children?

When I share about helping people like Patricia and her children, some people shout their support, while others claim I'm promoting some version of Christian socialism. But don't justice and kindness involve protecting and promoting rights and opportunities for all children and families, particularly those who have significant disadvantages?

Some may object to this line of reasoning, but again, consider the way that many Christians think about abortion. We know some unborn children are at a greater risk than others. Therefore, we work to ensure that all unborn children have an equal opportunity to live, without exception. But why would we work for children to be born, only to ignore them once their moms give birth? Certainly that's unjust (and absurd). Indeed, we care about children's lives not just in the womb but out of the womb. We care about their good in all of life, not just their first nine months. And we care about their parents, too, before and after they are pregnant.

We follow Jesus by doing justice for and showing kindness to single parents and children and families with significant disadvantages.

WHAT WILL OUR STORY BE?

Opportunities for us to do justice and love kindness abound in this fallen world. Recently I recorded a quick video to encourage a fifteen-year-old girl who has organized a community outreach group to fight sex trafficking in the Dallas–Fort Worth area. Moments after recording that video, I talked with a couple in our church who not only recently adopted a baby girl but also shared how her birth mom has become a meaningful part of their family. I have a message in my inbox from a friend who planted a church in an inner-city community where a six-year-old girl was recently shot. This friend and the members of his church are out on those streets sharing and showing God's love every day. And today I talked with a Pakistani sister in Christ who is teaching persecuted women and children to read.

In addition to opportunities to do justice individually, we have so many opportunities to work together for justice in the systems and structures around us. This is one of the many things I appreciate about Naomi and Dr. Zee. Yes, they adopted two wonderful boys into their family, one of whom I ran with in a 5k last weekend and could hardly keep up with even though he's only seven years old! Naomi and Dr. Zee organized this 5k as part of a community-wide fundraising effort to strengthen orphanages and raise awareness of policies and practices that address the root causes of orphan crises.

Do you remember the story I shared at the beginning of this chapter about standing with Naomi in a sea of street children? Naomi distinctly remembers seeing a young boy eating out of a trash can that day. That sight led her back to her hotel room that night, where she fell on her face and asked God what she could do to help that child and others like him. That prayer led her to start an after-school program that provides food for children in the name of Jesus, and it makes me wonder, *What if we all responded to injustice in the world like this?* What if instead of seeing injustice and moving on with our lives as we know them, we made it a practice to fall on our faces and ask God, "What are you calling us to do about this?" Surely we would discover that, whether in our own country or other countries, so many open doors are in front of us to do justice both individually and collectively.

Without question, Christians have often ignored these open doors and settled for (or even contributed to) injustice. This is part of why so many of us find ourselves in a state of disillusionment and doubt concerning the church. We have witnessed the destruction wrought by justice-ignoring, power-abusing, self-protecting, evil-tolerating churches, church leaders, and Christians in our country. An entire generation is turning to the world in search of justice and kindness because they don't see these things in the church.

But this doesn't have to be our story. Look back across the history of the church, and despite glaring flaws and failures, we see awesome displays of justice and kindness in the world. We see the church caring so much for the poor in the first century that "there was not a needy person among them" (Acts 4:34). We see Christians in subsequent centuries leading the way in outlawing infanticide, child abandonment, and abortion in the Roman Empire. We see the church working to stop barbarous gladiator battles, institute prison reforms, end the cruel punishment of criminals, justly punish pedophilia, rightly ban polygamy, promote education for the poor, and provide hospitals for the sick.

The church's efforts to do justice have continued around the world as Christian women and men have proclaimed the gospel while stopping widows from being burned alive with their husbands in India and helping outlaw the painful practice of binding young girls' feet in China. William Wilberforce led the way in abolishing the slave trade in England, and the African American church led the way in promoting civil rights in the United States. Throughout the history of the church, many of our forebearers in the faith have done justice and shown mercy while firmly holding to the gospel of Jesus. This is who we are designed by God to be, and this is what God has called us to do.

Again, various stories throughout history show the church doing harm in the name of Jesus, whether through colonialistic mission strategies or ignorant and insensitive mission efforts, and we mustn't repeat the errors of the past. But we also mustn't underestimate the impact of proclaiming the gospel and doing justice here and around the world. Robert Woodberry, a sociologist who did a decade's worth of research on the effect Christian missionaries had on the health of other nations, came to a stunning conclusion that he said landed on him like an atomic bomb. Specifically, he found that "the work of missionaries . . . turns out to be the single largest factor in ensuring the health of nations." What a statement. Listen to a summary of what Woodberry discovered:

> Areas where Protestant missionaries had a significant presence in the past are on average more economically developed today, with comparatively better health, lower infant mortality, lower corruption, greater literacy, higher educational attainment (especially for women), and more robust membership in nongovernmental associations.[7]

Woodberry's findings shouldn't be surprising to anyone who believes in the power of the gospel. For we know that when we proclaim Jesus *and* live and love according to his gospel, this good news changes lives, families, and nations.

So let's experience the good life. Let's do justice, love kindness, and walk humbly with our God. Let's hold orphans in our arms, help widows in our communities, provide for the poor in our cities, serve refugees in our country, host immigrants in our homes, rescue slaves from traffickers, visit people in prison, care for victims of abuse, come alongside moms and dads with unwanted pregnancies, and do multitudes of other things that are right for people as exemplified in God's character and expressed in God's Word. And let's do it all as we proclaim the name of Jesus in a world where billions of people still haven't even heard the good news about him.

5

RECTIFYING THE GREAT IMBALANCE

Gospel Poverty and Our Life Purpose

There's a reason not a lot of people live in the Amazon. The world's largest rain forest is also one of its most aggressive physical environments—certainly the most aggressive I've ever experienced.

After flying on a puddle jumper into a remote village, a small group of us walked down to the Amazon River, where a couple of long, motorized canoes awaited us. We climbed in, each of us carrying a small backpack with filtered water bottles, miscellaneous snacks, a change of clothes, and a small camping hammock. We started down the river with a couple of indigenous men who would be our guides and become our friends on the journey, and we soon found ourselves walled in by dense undergrowth and towering trees. Occasionally, a clearing opened to reveal homes nestled together on the riverbanks. The dwellings were made of plaster with metal roofs. But as we traveled deeper into the interior, any signs of village life became few and far between.

Once deep in the heart of the rain forest, we arrived at the starting point for our trek. Our guides beached and secured the boats; then we hoisted our packs and started walking.

Within seconds, we were swarmed by more species of biting and stinging insects than I knew existed. And those bugs were hungry! I wore long pants and a long-sleeved shirt, but somehow they still made their way through my clothes to feast on my flesh. I'd been told to spray a lot of DEET on my clothes, which I'd done with utmost care, but evidently, these bugs eat DEET for breakfast.

The bugs were a nuisance, for sure, but I was far more concerned about the jaguars and venomous snakes I'd read about in preparation for this trip. Were they hiding in the thick brush, just waiting to strike? The indigenous guides (who, by the way, were trekking in sandals and shorts, often without shirts) tried to encourage us. "Don't worry," they said through a translator. "The most dangerous animals sleep during the day."

That was comforting—during the day. But it didn't exactly alleviate my anxiety about the night, when the jaguars and snakes would be most awake and I would be least conscious, dangling in a hammock like dinner on a platter.

After hiking for hours through the forest, we arrived at our campsite and hung our hammocks between trees. (With tarantulas and other critters crawling around, the ground wasn't an ideal place to sleep.) When it was time to retire for the night, we climbed into the cocoons of our hammocks, pulled mosquito nets over our bodies, and cinched them behind our heads. While I was thankful for the protection from the bugs, I knew that net wasn't posing any threat to a jaguar.

As I closed my eyes and prayed against jaguar hunger, I discovered the sanctifying experience of simply falling asleep in the Amazon. Lying there in the pitch-black dark, you can't see your hand in front of your face, but you can hear *everything*—and the Amazon comes alive at night. You hear rustling above and below, the whines, buzzes, and clicks of insects nearby, and the lunatic roaring of howler monkeys in the distance. I prayed one prayer over and over again until I fell asleep: "Oh God, please get me through this night."

The following morning, I woke with boundless gratitude for daylight breaking through the trees. I'd made it, and so had all my fellow travelers. An hour or so later, we were on our way.

Each day, we hiked, and each evening, we sat around a campfire with our guides—truly amazing men who call the rain forest home. Together we ate noodles cooked over an open fire. To the soundtrack of crackling wood and the jungle life all around us, these men shared fascinating stories about their families, their ancestry, and their way of life in one of the most remote places on earth.

One night, after we'd listened raptly to their tales, Bieto, one of our guides, asked me whether I had any good stories to share. I was glad to oblige, and I told them four short stories from Mark 4–5 about how the Creator of this rain forest had come to the world as a man named Jesus and how he had power over nature, evil spirits, disease, and death.

The following night around the fire, another of the guides, Luan, recalled the stories I'd shared. "When you were telling those stories," he said, "I had an unusual feeling inside, like my heart was beating out of my chest."

"These stories have that kind of effect on people," I said. Then my fellow trekkers and I took turns sharing the larger story of the Bible—the good news of how Jesus lived a sinless life, died a sacrificial death for sinners, and rose from the grave in victory over death.

On the last night of the trek, Bieto spoke up again. "When you share these stories about Jesus, I feel like I have a dirty heart. Is there a way my heart can be made clean?"

"That's the good news about Jesus," I said. "The reason he came was to give us a totally new heart."

That's when Luan said words that I will never forget. "These stories about Jesus are so good," he said with wonderment. "And they seem so important. I just don't understand why we and our tribes and all our ancestors before us have never heard them until now."

I'd like to ask you to consider Luan's question: Why do *you* think approximately 3.2 billion men, women, and children like these men and their families have never heard the good news of Jesus?[1]

My contention in this chapter is simple. While many factors contribute to "gospel poverty" in jungles, villages, and megacities around the world, one of the primary reasons—if not *the* primary reason—that billions of people remain unreached by the gospel is that *the global purpose of God has always faced resistance from the nationalistic people of God*.

From the nation of Israel in the Old Testament, to the early church in the New Testament, to the current church in the United States, people of God have continually desired the preservation of *their* nation more than the proclamation of the gospel in *all* nations. And just as generations of God's people before us needed to do, God is calling us to place less priority on our beloved home country—a country that will one day fall—and more priority on a global kingdom that will last forever. Not only is doing so urgent for billions of people in need of the gospel; it is also necessary in order to overcome sickness in the church.

THE PURPOSE OF YOUR LIFE

At this point, you might be thinking that you love God but, well, "missions work" around the world isn't your cup of tea, so this chapter isn't for you. You're thankful for those who *are* called to this kind of work, and you wish them the best. And if you're thinking this way, then either you aren't a Christian or you have a serious misunderstanding about what it means to follow Christ.

Let me explain.

When I was in college, I began to see that the pages of the Bible point to a clear conclusion: The gospel is not just for me and people like me, but it is for all people in all nations. Just look at how the Bible ends—with a scene in the book of Revelation where people from every nation, tribe, and language gather around God's throne and enjoy his presence for eternity (7:9–17). I recognized that *this* outcome is God's ultimate purpose, and I realized that if I'm a part of the people of God, then this should be my ultimate purpose too. If the train of history is headed toward this destination and if I wanted to live for what matters most, then I needed to jump aboard this train. I needed to do whatever I could so that people from every nation would enjoy God's salvation.

In my mind, there was only one way to do that. I needed to become a missionary to another nation. But there's where my thinking needed correction, and that correction came courtesy of a man named Dr. Jerry Rankin.

At the time, Dr. Rankin led the International Mission Board, which, as I mentioned earlier, comprises thousands of missionaries around the world. When he visited the graduate school I was attending after college, I was invited to take him to breakfast. The night before that breakfast, I told Heather that I planned to tell Dr. Rankin we were ready to move overseas as missionaries. She was in full support, and the next morning, we prayed together before I left for my appointment.

At breakfast, Dr. Rankin and I ordered our food, and I began pouring out my heart. "Dr. Rankin, I see God's plan for his glory to be enjoyed and exalted in all nations, and I see the need for the gospel in so many nations, so my wife and I are ready to go."

He listened thoughtfully, then said nothing for an awkward sixty seconds. When he broke his silence, he encouraged my heart for the nations but strangely didn't encourage me to pack my bags and move. Instead, he spent the rest of breakfast telling me about the need for pastors to lead churches in ways that help spread the gospel to places it hasn't gone.

I was so confused. When I got back home, Heather eagerly asked, "How'd it go?"

"I . . . I think the leader of this missions organization just talked me out of becoming a missionary," I said.

A look of disappointment came across her face, as if I'd blown the job interview and bungled our plans. But try as I might, I couldn't think of what I'd said wrong to Dr. Rankin.

In time, and the more I processed that conversation, the more thankful I became. A new way of thinking was emerging, one that hadn't existed in my mind until that breakfast. For on that morning, I learned that there is a type of person who is extremely passionate about the spread of the gospel to all nations but who doesn't become a missionary. Do you know what I discovered that type of person is called?

A Christian.

After all, the Spirit of God is *passionate* about all nations knowing the love of God. This means that if God's Spirit dwells in you, then you will be *passionate* about all nations knowing the love of God. To be a follower of Jesus is to live with zeal for all the nations to know Jesus. The spread of the gospel among all the nations is not a program for a chosen few. It's actually the purpose for which we all have breath and the end toward which all of history is headed (see Revelation 7:9–10).

(I'd like to ask you to re-read that paragraph above. Slowly. Let it really soak in before you move on. This is the purpose of God in the world and for each of our lives—*essential* for understanding what it means to follow Jesus—and I'm convinced that most Christians in our country are completely missing it.)

A COUPLE OF CLARIFICATIONS

This chapter is about the overarching purpose of God in history and our lives: to spread the gospel and glory of God among all the nations. As we think together about this purpose, I want to clarify a couple of things.

First, when the Bible talks about nations, it's referring to specific ethnic groups or people groups, thousands of which exist in the world today. It isn't referring to the geopolitical entities we call nations today (after all, most nations today, including the United States, didn't exist when the Bible was written). However, for the purposes of this chapter and specifically for applying these truths to Christians in the United States, most of my references to nations will be either to the nation of Israel as it existed in biblical times or to the approximately two hundred geopolitical entities that we call nations today, including the United States.

Second, I want to state unequivocally that I am a proud citizen of my nation. I love living in metro Washington, D.C., the capital of my country. My family and I still enjoy walking among the monuments downtown. I think about a recent trip with our kids to the World War II Memorial when a bus full of veterans arrived. In an unplanned and poignant scene, we formed a line with others along the sidewalk, clapping and cheering in respectful esteem as these veterans and their families walked slowly or were pushed in wheelchairs toward the memorial. I told my kids, "These soldiers gave their lives to protect and promote the freedoms we enjoy every day. We don't ever need to take who they are and what they did for granted." And I don't.

I love being in a church where many veterans and military members attend and serve as leaders alongside others who help make our nation's government function. I have the highest respect for one of our pastors who served for decades as a Navy SEAL, participated in countless missions around the world, and saw far too many of his comrades not come home. As I was writing this chapter, Pastor Todd (as he's known by so many in the church) spoke at a lunch to honor former and current military members in our church and community. He and others like him are heroes in our house.

Obedience to Jesus's command to make disciples of all nations doesn't mean we don't love our own nation. But we need to ask ourselves: Is it possible that pride in our own nation can keep us from living for God's purpose in all nations? Absolutely, it is. And it's been that way from ancient times.

THE JONAH IN US

Consider a national hero in Israel named Jonah. During the reign of King Jeroboam, God sent Jonah to tell the king to shore up a long section of Israel's northern border to strengthen their defenses against their mortal enemy, Assyria. The Assyrians were known for their immorality, arrogance, and brutality in war. But when Jonah delivered God's warning to the king, Jeroboam solidified Israel's defenses and the nation was protected (2 Kings 14:23–27).

Imagine Jonah's surprise, then, when God came to him and said, "Now go and preach in Nineveh, the capital city of Assyria." In other words, "Go and preach God's word to your mortal enemy—the cruel nation that has threatened to overtake Israel."

What was Jonah's response? He ran away from God and his plans. At the port city of Joppa, Jonah booked passage for Tarshish, a distant land in the opposite direction from Nineveh. Yet God came after him.

What good news. Aren't you glad to know that, even in our obstinance, God's people can't outrun God's grace? Aren't you thankful that God's capacity to forgive is greater than our capacity to sin?

You (and most kids in church) remember how God got ahold of Jonah. A violent storm blew up, and realizing he was the reason for the storm, Jonah volunteered to be thrown overboard. But not long after he hit the water, a giant fish swallowed him whole, and he spent the next three days inside the fish's digestive tract praying for deliverance. When God answered, the fish spat the bedraggled prophet onto shore.

Then God came again to Jonah and said, "Go and preach in Nineveh." This time, Jonah obeyed.

Jonah preached a simple eight-word sermon, calling the Ninevites to repent and receive the mercy of God. To the shock of most, the people of Nineveh did exactly that. The Bible records that this cruel people believed God, called for a fast, and turned from their sin. And it wasn't just a few of them. It was everyone, "from the greatest of them to the least of them" (Jonah 3:5).

But Jonah wasn't surprised. He'd known this was going to happen, and he was mad about it. Listen to his complaint to God about the Assyrians' repentance:

> O Lord, is not this what I said when I was yet in my country? That is why I made haste to flee to Tarshish; for I knew that you are a gracious God and merciful, slow to anger and abounding in steadfast love, and relenting from disaster. Therefore now, O Lord, please take my life from me, for it is better for me to die than to live. (4:2–3)

What an astounding statement from the person entrusted with the responsibility to proclaim God's love. Jonah would rather die than see the enemy of his nation saved!

Instead of leading the repentant Ninevites in prayer and worship, Jonah sat down outside the city and pouted, wishing God would rain down judgment on the Assyrians. But God didn't rain down judgment on anyone. Instead, he graciously provided a large plant to shade Jonah from the heat. The story still wasn't over, though. Before long, God allowed the plant to wither and die, and Jonah found himself upset all over again.

This is where the story of Jonah ends—not with a happily-ever-after moment but with a haunting question from God for Jonah and, by implication, for all God's people: "You care about one plant that protects you from the heat of the sun. Should I not care about whole nations in need of my salvation?" (see verses 10–11).

THE GREAT IMBALANCE

Surely I'm not like Jonah, we say to ourselves. But let's not draw this conclusion too quickly. Let's at least examine our hearts with a few simple questions. Pause and answer these honestly:

- Have you ever wanted your way more than you have wanted God's will?
- Are you inclined to settle for the comforts of people and places that are familiar to you instead of paying a cost to go to people and places that are foreign to you? Espe-

cially if those people are also threatening to you or perceived as your enemies?

- How often do you pray for and desire the good of other
countries that might be considered enemies of the
United States?

- Is it possible for you to know about the character of
God yet not show the compassion of God to others?

- Are you prone to disconnect the mercy of God in your
life from the mission of God in the world?

- Do you sometimes care more about your earthly desires
than others' eternal destinies?

- What do you truly want more: a comfortable life in
your nation or the spread of the gospel in all nations?

If we're going to accurately answer these questions, we
need to look at the evidence in our lives, as well as our
churches.

For example, you might say, no, you don't want a comfortable life in your nation more than the spread of the gospel in
all nations. But how much of your time, energy, resources,
and attention are you giving to seeing the gospel spread to
billions of unreached people? Compare your answer to that
question with the amount of time, energy, resources, and attention you're giving to making your life comfortable.

I can't answer that question for you, but I can answer it for
us as the church in the United States. It's all there in the numbers. American Christians spend most of our money on ourselves, and we give a relatively small percentage to our
churches and various other ministries. Out of this money we
give to our churches, we spend the overwhelming majority on

church buildings, events, and programs that make church more comfortable for and appealing to us. Only a small portion of our giving goes toward what we call "missions work" outside our country.

Yet, of our giving toward "missions work," most Christians have no idea what percentage actually goes to spreading the gospel among the billions of people in other nations who have never heard it.

The answer?

Approximately 1 percent. (It's true—we've done the research.[2])

In addition to the hundreds of billions of dollars we in the church spend on ourselves, approximately 99 percent of our giving to "missions work" goes to places like Latin America and sub-Saharan Africa where the gospel has already gone. In other words, even when we think we're giving to missions, we're actually ignoring the billions of people who most need the gospel.

Jesus said, "Where your treasure is, there your heart will be also" (Matthew 6:21). It's obvious that the American church doesn't have a heart to get the gospel to those who have never heard it. Otherwise, according to Jesus, our dollars would show it.

What's worse, the number of people who haven't heard the gospel is increasing every day through population growth. This means that unless we rectify this great imbalance in what we're giving to and living for, more people than ever will continue to die and go to hell without hearing about the saving love of Jesus. We're talking about billions of people going to hell for all of eternity while we spend our resources on our American churches and our American way of life.[3] Surely true followers of Jesus are not content with this.

CHANGING OUR DAILY LIVES

Look closely at what Jesus told his followers, and think about the implications for your life if you claim to be a Christian. Jesus's first command to his disciples was "Follow me, and I will make you fishers of men" (Matthew 4:19). He said repeatedly, "If anyone would come after me, let him deny himself and take up his cross daily and follow me" (Luke 9:23). His final command was specific and clear: "Go . . . and make disciples of all nations" (Matthew 28:19). Not "Come, be baptized, and ride things out in one location." Not "Say a prayer, go to church, read your Bible when you have time, be the best person you can be, and throw your leftover change to the nations in need of the gospel." Not "Syncretize your American lifestyle with what it means to be a #blessed Christian." No, it's clear from the Bible: Being a disciple of Jesus means letting his global purpose drive everything you think, desire, and do in your family, work, and church, for the rest of your life. Which means however and wherever Jesus wants to lead your life.

Are you willing to pack your bags and move to the Middle East to make disciples there? If not, according to Luke 9:23, you're either not a Christian or you don't understand Christianity. Because Christians have surrendered the right to determine the direction of their lives. "If anyone would come after me, he must deny himself," Jesus says, meaning the starting point for a Christian is dying to yourself and living for Jesus's purpose, no matter what that means or where he leads. A willingness to make disciples in the Middle East, or any nation, isn't a mark of a mature Christian; it's the most basic, elementary expectation of every Christian.

Regardless of where Jesus leads us to live, this purpose changes the way we think and pray every day. Jesus told us to plead continually for God's name to be hallowed and God's kingdom to advance among all the nations (Matthew 6:9–10). He told us to pray earnestly for more workers in fields around the world that are ripe for harvest (Matthew 9:37–38). He told us to pray for open doors for the spread of the gospel to more people in more places (Colossians 4:2–4). This is how Christians pray.

In our day, God has given us technology to help us do this like never before. We can use tools like Stratus.Earth to understand the spiritual and physical needs of the nations or Joshua Project's Unreached of the Day app to learn about and intercede daily and specifically for the billions of people without the gospel. Prayer is so simple yet so neglected. Before we even get out of bed in the morning, you and I can join in what God is doing for the spread of the gospel in Iran, Libya, and Saudi Arabia. Can you think of a better way to start a day?

I think of one couple, Stephen and Jamie, who I had the joy of helping send out to make disciples and multiply churches in a difficult and dangerous part of the world. Stephen and Jamie enlisted a small group from the church to faithfully pray for them and those they were trying to reach. As they went and worked in this far-off nation with little access to the gospel, sisters and brothers eagerly awaited their updates.

"Pray for Amid; we're about to share the gospel with him," Stephen would text, and the group would pray. "Pray for Amid again; he's getting closer to faith." This went on for years, until one day Amid came to faith in Jesus.

As God worked in response to his people praying, this story repeated itself at different times in different ways. The result? Not only did God hear and answer prayers for people in need of Jesus, but more and more people in the church also realized the role they could (and should) play every day in the spread of the gospel among the nations. They came to see that this is what prayer is for. In the words of John Piper, prayer is a "walkie-talkie . . . for the accomplishment of a wartime mission." He writes:

> It is as though the field commander (Jesus) called in the troops, gave them a crucial mission (go and bear fruit), handed each of them a personal transmitter coded to the frequency of the general's headquarters, and said, "Comrades, the general has a mission for you. He aims to see it accomplished. And to that end he has authorized me to give each of you personal access to him through these transmitters. If you stay true to his mission and seek his victory first, he will always be as close as your transmitter, to give tactical advice and to send air cover when you need it.

Then Piper describes how millions of Christians have missed God's purpose for this walkie-talkie, choosing to "rig it up as an intercom in our houses and cabins and boats and cars—not to call in firepower for conflict with a mortal enemy but to ask for more comforts in the den."[4] We are wasting the privilege of prayer if we're not using it for God's purpose: the spread of his glory among all the nations.

Wealth for the Gospel

Recognizing God's ultimate purpose also changes the way we—as the people in whom the Spirit of Jesus dwells—use our money. After all, God has put us in one of the wealthiest countries in the history of the world. Has God really done this just so that we can acquire more and newer and better possessions that won't last? Or has God given us relative wealth for the spread of his worldwide worship?

This is why Radical (the organization) started an initiative called Urgent to identify places around the world where spiritual and physical needs most intersect. Put another way, these are places where people are least reached by the gospel and experience the most physical suffering. We wanted to make a way for Christians and churches to rectify this great imbalance by giving to faithful gospel work on the front lines of the most urgent needs in the world.

The opportunities for you and me to be involved in work like this abound. I receive regular stories from Urgent workers spreading the gospel in places like North Korea, Somalia, Sudan, Vietnam, and Bhutan. I recently had lunch with a group of sisters and brothers working in India, Pakistan, and Afghanistan, where they are leading people to Jesus, planting churches, caring for the poor, defending the oppressed, and working to free those imprisoned for their faith. I sat at the table humbled and overjoyed by the opportunity to be a part of a global family taking the greatest news in history to the hardest places in the world for the very first time.

I love not only experiencing this joy but also seeing it in the faces of other Christians in the United States when they begin to realize the opportunities we have to be a part of what God is doing all over the world, particularly among people who are unreached by the gospel. I recently received an email from a college student eagerly describing her plans to use her small income to spread the gospel in the Himalayas. Another email from a multimillionaire shared how he is gladly giving away millions of dollars for the spread of the gospel across North Africa and the Middle East, and he is now expanding his efforts to other places.

I love this! It doesn't matter whether you're a student living off ramen in a college dorm room or you're an executive raking in the dough—by God's grace, we all have a unique and meaningful part to play in God's purpose among the nations! And being a Christian means stewarding our possessions for this purpose.

When God Brings the Nations to Us

It's not just about praying and giving, of course. Christians personally go and make disciples among all nations. And you and I can start right outside our front doors.

Millions of people have immigrated from other nations to the United States, some permanently and others temporarily, including a million international students on college campuses. In the county in Georgia where I grew up, the foreign-born population has more than doubled in the past fifteen years alone. Around the country, large percentages of immigrants have come from places where the gospel hasn't gone, evidenced by the Hindu temples and Muslim mosques being erected in many communities.

Sadly, as I mentioned earlier, research shows that evangelical Christians are some of the Americans who are most upset about these newcomers. I'm not at all presuming there aren't significant concerns with our country's immigration legislation (or the lack thereof). But out of all people in our country, shouldn't followers of Jesus be first to rejoice that, in a very real sense, God is bringing multitudes who have been far from him near to us in order that we might share the good news about Jesus with them?

I've seen this play out where I live. In fact, I think about two weeks when I saw this reality unfold three times.

After worship one Sunday, I was standing in the lobby when a Middle Eastern woman named Celine came over to me. She seemed extremely nervous. She said that she'd never been to a church before and that her family wouldn't approve of her being there. But she'd had a dream the night before where someone in the dream told her to come to our church and listen.

"When you spoke about Jesus," Celine said, "I knew immediately that I wanted to place my trust in him." I connected her with one of the women leaders of our church, and not long thereafter, Celine was baptized as a follower of Jesus.

The very next Sunday, a member of our church I'll call Jasmine, who is of Persian descent and speaks Farsi, was sitting in her car in the parking lot, about to come inside, when a young woman named Ariana knocked on the window. Jasmine rolled down the window to ask whether she could help.

"I have never been here before," Ariana said, "and I don't know where to go. All I know is that I had a dream last night, and a man in the dream said I need to come here. Can you help me?"

Jasmine smiled, immediately got out of the car to speak with her, and learned that Ariana was Persian-born and spoke Farsi. Jasmine shared the gospel with her that day in her heart language, and before long, Ariana was baptized.

The following week, I found myself needing to take a last-minute flight. The only flight I could find was at five-thirty in the morning at an airport about an hour away from my house. I woke up before three, groggily scheduled an Uber ride, and, when the time came, climbed into a car with a driver from the Middle East named Hasim. We exchanged small talk, and Hasim asked me what I did for a living. I told him I was a pastor, then watched in the rearview mirror as his eyes lit up. "I must tell you a story," he said.

"As a Muslim, we believe that Jesus was a prophet and a great man, but not God in the flesh like Christians believe. But one night I had a dream, and I saw a tiny baby who was speaking to me as clearly as an adult might speak. The baby looked directly at me and said, 'Do not question or underestimate what God can do.'" Then Hasim asked me, "Do you know what this dream means?"

I smiled and said, "Hasim, I don't claim to be a dream interpreter, but I know exactly what this one means." My middle name is Joseph, after all. (See Genesis 40–41 if that reference doesn't make sense.)

I continued. "Hasim, I know this for certain. God loves you, and God has done the unthinkable. God has come to this world—to you and to me—to pay the price for sin by dying on a cross." I knew that Muslims deny that Jesus died on a cross, but I kept going. "Jesus is God in the flesh, and he has died on the cross to make it possible for you to be forgiven of your sins and to be restored to relationship with God."

Tears welled up in Hasim's eyes, and he apologized as he wiped his face. I assured him no apologies were necessary as long as he kept his eyes on the road! He smiled and said, "I can't believe this conversation is happening." I sat there in the back smiling, wondering whether this Uber might be a chariot with an Ethiopian official. (See Acts 8 if that reference doesn't make sense either.)

We arrived at the airport, and I asked, "Do you believe this, Hasim? Do you believe that Jesus is God in the flesh, who came to die for your sins? And are you willing to follow him, starting today, in your life?"

"Yes, I believe this," he said, "and I want to follow Jesus."

Indeed, Acts 17:26–27 is true: God is sovereignly orchestrating the movement of people from different nations—immigrants and refugees alike—so that they might find Jesus.

But take my word, if you share this truth from God's Word, no matter how many times you explain that you're not advocating for particular political positions on immigration or refugees, you will be labeled a leftist whose ideology is harmful to the future of our country. It's astonishing how zeal for our nation—and even specific political policies in it—overpowers passion to share the gospel with people God is bringing to us from other nations.

Leverage Your Life

Throughout my years as a pastor, I have seen so many good people resist any call to spread the gospel in other countries. We have enough needs and problems here, some say, so we should just focus on our country. And to be clear, the Bible never teaches that all Christians should pack their bags and move to another country. But in a world where billions don't even have access to the gospel, surely God is calling a lot more of us to go to them. And even if we don't go, biblically he's calling all of us to be a part of helping spread the gospel to them.

This is all the more true when we realize that, with globalization, urbanization, ease of travel, and new technology, we have more opportunities than ever before to spread the gospel to all nations. The apostle Paul could have only dreamed about the privileges we have. It took him months to sail from one city to the next. We can circle the world in less than a day. He had to write letters that would take weeks to be delivered. With the evolution of the internet and social media, combined with advancements in translation software, not to mention the emergence of the metaverse, we can communicate with people around the world in real time—from a device in our pockets!

I recently met with a group of well-known innovators, influencers, and leaders in different sectors of society, from business and technology to sports and entertainment. All of them are followers of Jesus, and together we explored the myriad ways we can leverage the opportunities before us to reach those who haven't heard the gospel. What is possible through all the platforms and resources God has placed at our disposal today? It's exhilarating to consider the historically unique opportunities God has given us to accomplish his purpose in the world.

Just think of the job opportunities that exist in places where the gospel hasn't gone. In the past few months, a husband in our church took a job in West Africa and moved his family there. Why? For the sake of spreading the gospel among unreached people. A single mom in our church took a job in South Asia and moved there with her son for the same purpose. We have many others in a pipeline looking to follow their lead. I'm seeing high school and college students get degrees that will open doors for them to spread the gospel in other nations. I think of a nursing student who graduated from college and took a job in the Middle East, where she is now in charge of nursing in her hospital and shares the gospel with people every week. Or I think of Hugh, a follower of Jesus whose lumber business is expanding to countries around the world, creating wide-open avenues not just for commerce but for the spread of the gospel to people who have never heard it.

I could give example after example, but do you see what's happening? God has rigged this system (i.e., the world!) for the spread of his glory. Nations without the gospel (many of which are opposed to the gospel) are actually (and unknowingly) funding the spread of the gospel to themselves. The question is, Will we, as God's people, open our eyes and leverage our lives to accomplish the purpose for which God has left us in the world?

ETERNITY ON THE LINE

We need to see the tendency in each of our hearts to resist this global purpose, just as God's people have done throughout history. From the beginning, in Genesis 11, people refused to scatter for the spread of God's fame, choosing to stay in one place and build a name for themselves. Or consider Isaiah 56, when God established an entire court in the temple for the Gentiles to come and worship him, but by Mark 11, God's people were setting up shop in that court to make profit for themselves while the Gentiles went to hell.

As the gospel began spreading in the book of Acts, Peter was criticized for preaching to non-Jews. In fact, the predominantly Jewish church wanted to create barriers to keep the Gentiles from entering the church, hoping to reserve the good news for their own nation. Even the disciples' question for Jesus at the beginning of Acts—"Lord, will you at this time restore the kingdom to Israel?" (1:6)—shows that they were still thinking about their own people more than a kingdom that would expand to all people.

We shouldn't be surprised by any of this. There is an adversary in this world who doesn't want the gospel to go to all the nations. He wants as many souls as possible in hell, and he is diabolically committed to keeping the nations from hearing about the kingdom of heaven. I use this language with great intentionality and solemnity. Again, we're talking about more than 3,200,000,000 people (and increasing every day) who are separated from God by their sin, who are on a road that leads to an eternal hell, and who can't be saved from this fate unless they hear and believe the gospel.

God, help us feel the weight of this reality.

Why are we not talking about unreached people all the time in our lives, families, and churches today? Why are we not praying, giving, going, sending, and sacrificing in every way we can to spread the gospel among all the nations? We certainly wouldn't say this out loud, but could it be that we've grown accustomed to a church culture in our country that seems pretty content with turning a blind eye and a deaf ear to billions of people on their way to hell who have never even heard the truth about how to go to heaven? In other words, Could it be that we have actually become comfortable with missing the heart of Christ?

It's no wonder we're disillusioned. No matter how much we pretend, we can't expect to experience the full satisfaction of Jesus's presence with us if we're ignoring his purpose for us.

And of course we're divided. Wouldn't our discussions—and our perspectives on disagreements—change in the church if we collectively took the time to look into the faces of suffering refugees in Syria and starving families in Sudan who are on a road that leads to eternal suffering and have never heard how Jesus wants them to have eternal life? Wouldn't we be less inclined to fight one another and more inclined to fight for them?

Wouldn't this also change the way we're training the next generation? I recently saw a video on social media of a girl I'll call Kristen, who was soon to graduate high school. Kristen is a member of the Church of Jesus Christ of Latter-Day Saints, a group commonly known as Mormons. Traditionally, nearly every Mormon student who graduates high school spends the following year somewhere away from home sharing the teachings of Joseph Smith. To be clear, theirs is not the biblical gospel that saves but a counterfeit gospel that condemns.

In the video, Kristen was at home reading a letter she'd received informing her where her upcoming mission assignment would take her. As she read it, she shook with nervous excitement. When she came to the part detailing her assignment, her face lit up with a shining smile. Immediately the camera panned out and revealed her family and a host of friends who had gathered to cheer in celebration.

Why is this? Why is a teenage member of a cult—a cult with a counterfeit and condemning gospel—more excited about and committed to going to the nations than Christians are, even though we have the true gospel of Jesus Christ? And why are we as the church—the true bride of Christ— not raising up the next generation with the expectation that they will take the gospel to the nations as we passionately cheer them on?

I think about all the students I spend time with in our church and on college campuses. Many tell me that the greatest hindrance to taking the gospel to the nations is actually their Christian parents. Parents are telling children to study, practice sports, and learn instruments, and we're overseeing hours upon hours of their days in front of screens. We prioritize taking them all over the place for all kinds of activities, telling them they need a good education so they can get a good degree, find a good job, make good money, and have a good family with a good retirement. These aren't unworthy concerns. But in the middle of it all, we need to ask a more significant question: How are we training the next generation to accomplish the Great Commission?

Or consider potentially more significant questions than that: Are parents and other adults, young and old alike, showing the next generation what commitment to the Great Commission looks like in action? Do today's students see in their dads and moms, and men and women around them in church, a zeal for God's glory and love for all people, including those who might be perceived as enemies? Do they see modeled before them an all-consuming passion and vision for the proclamation of the gospel in all nations? Because this is the vision of Christianity we see in the Bible, and it's totally different from the vision being cast in our country.

It's time for us as the people of God to recalibrate our priorities and realize our purpose. Whether you're a student, a senior adult, or anywhere in between, it is right to praise God for the gifts he has given you and me in a country that has freedom, resources, and opportunity like no other in the world. It is good to pass on these gifts to the next generation of Americans. Yet it is infinitely more important, satisfying, and unifying to give our lives to passing on the good news of Jesus to the Luans, Bietos, and *three billion others* whose eternity hinges on hearing and believing the gospel.

6

GOD OUR OBSESSION

The Great End of the Gospel

I was sitting on the front row of a packed church in Seoul, South Korea, looking over my notes as I prepared to preach. When one of the pastors of the church took center stage and started speaking, I barely paid attention. Until *it* happened.

Without warning, a roar of voices filled the room. Startled, I looked around as everyone yelled what sounded like "Ju-yeo!" Then they started speaking and shouting, some with heads bowed, others with hands raised, most with eyes closed, and all with passionate zeal. It seemed like every person was pleading or crying in desperation.

I turned to my friend and translator and asked, "What's going on?"

"They're praying," he said. "What sounds like 'Ju-yeo!' is 'Lord!' in English."

"What did the pastor say that led them to pray like this?" I asked. "Is something wrong?"

"The pastor didn't share anything unusual. This is just how they pray."

This scene of desperation didn't stop. They kept praying and praying and praying. My friend explained some of what he was hearing: "Some are praising God. Some are thanking God for his grace in their lives and families and the church. Others are confessing sin. Others are interceding for people in need."

"How long will this last?" I asked.

"Until they're finished," he answered. "On Friday nights and into Saturday mornings, they pray all night long instead of sleeping. Others gather at four every morning to pray for an hour or two or three."

I looked around the room and realized that the crowd hadn't assembled that night because they were excited about hearing the latest, greatest Korean Christian band. They weren't gathering because they were eager to hear me preach either. A crowd of people had crammed into that building because they were zealous to meet with God.

Not once in the forty years I'd been a part of churches had I experienced desperate prayer like this—and half that time I was *leading* in the church. Not once had I met with a congregation at four in the morning to pray for two or three hours, much less every morning. And not once had I prayed or led the church to pray together all night long without sleep.

Listening to that roar of prayers—these urgent, passionate voices lifted to God—I had a realization. I am a part of and a leader in an American church culture that loves doing so many things: engaging in programs and activities, meeting to discuss ideas and plans, and creating events and entertainment, concerts and conferences, or entire churches that revolve around charismatic speakers and musicians. But we rarely come together with zeal just to meet with God.

It's as if we in the United States have looked at God as a means to all these other ends instead of seeking and being satisfied in God as the end. As I near the conclusion of this book, I believe this is one of the primary reasons—if not *the* primary reason—the American church is in its current state. For far too long, an American gospel has fueled desires for all sorts of things other than the one thing—or, more appropriately put, the One—we most need. And I believe this means our greatest need moving forward—over and above everything else—is simply to cry out in individual and collective desperation for God and God alone as the prize of our lives.

ONE THING

God himself is the end—the greatest gift, the ultimate goal, and the cherished prize—of the biblical gospel. This is evident in the Bible from cover to cover. Imagine Adam, the first person in the book of Genesis, raised from a pile of dust to stand before God. For the first time, a human being was conscious, able to see and think and feel and move. God said to him, "You see that dirt. That's what you were a second ago. I just breathed life into your lungs, and here you are, with me." Adam looked to God in awe and began walking with his Creator in uninhibited worship. The beauty of this garden scene soon included Eve as this breathtaking truth unfolded: Men and women were made to experience life to the full in pure, unadulterated communion with God.

This awe, worship, and perfect communion didn't last forever, though. Sin destroyed it, creating a separation between people and God that lasts until the book of Revelation, when heaven comes down to earth and the Bible declares once again, "Behold, the dwelling place of God is with man. He will dwell with them, and they will be his people, and God himself will be with them as their God" (21:3). Apparently, what makes heaven so great isn't the gold streets or beautiful mansions we have so often imagined in our American gospel, as if God is trying to compete with (or outdo) our economic prosperity. What makes heaven so great is the reality that followers of Jesus are finally and perfectly with God, the One who is better than all the best things of this world put together.

The entire story of the Bible from Genesis 1 to Revelation 22 is the story of women and men yearning for this kind of communion with God. The psalmist expressed it well:

> One thing have I asked of the LORD,
>   that will I seek after:
> that I may dwell in the house of the LORD
>   all the days of my life,
> to gaze upon the beauty of the LORD
>   and to inquire in his temple. (27:4)

"*One thing*," he said. More than anything else, he wanted to be with God. He just wanted to look at him. He just wanted to speak to him. All of God is all he wanted.

Let's pause to ask, Is that all we want?

Or do we want a lot of other things? Let's be honest. Is God the *end*—the gift, the goal, the prize of our lives—or simply a *means* to a host of other highly desirable outcomes?

SEEKING, THIRSTING, FAINTING

I see this picture of God as *the* prize of our lives so clearly in Psalm 63. Listen to David's language there:

> O God, you are my God; earnestly I seek you;
>   my soul thirsts for you;
> my flesh faints for you,
>   as in a dry and weary land where there is no water.
>   (verse 1)

Doesn't that sound like God was the *one thing* David wanted and earnestly sought?

The word *seek* in that passage is beautifully poetic, related to the Hebrew noun for "dawn," creating the picture of a man who, from the moment he rises in the morning, thirsts for God like he's in a desert and desperate for water. Later in the same psalm, David wrote that his soul longed for God like his body longed for food (verse 5). Such longing dominated David's day late into the night. He said to God, "I remember you upon my bed, and meditate on you in the watches of the night" (verse 6).

David sounds pretty obsessed, doesn't he? Like a boy who can't stop thinking about the girl he loves. Like an addict who's convinced that if he could only have that *one thing*, then he would be satisfied.

The farther you read in the Bible, the more you discover that obsession with God is what faith is all about. Think about Paul's words in Philippians: "For to me to live is Christ, and to die is gain" (1:21). What a declaration. Paul couldn't wait to die, because he knew that would mean he'd be with God. That's why he wrote, "My desire is to depart and be with Christ, for that is far better" (verse 23). The language here is like when I'm out of town on a long trip and I send a text to my wife, saying, "I miss you so much, and I can't wait to be away from here and back home with you." Paul said, "That's the way I feel about Jesus. I just want to be with him!"

Obsession is fundamental to being a follower of Jesus. In Luke 14:26, Jesus said to a crowd of people, "If anyone comes to me and does not hate his own father and mother and wife and children and brothers and sisters, yes, and even his own life, he cannot be my disciple." Obviously, we know from all of Scripture that we're commanded to honor our fathers and mothers and care for our children and families. But Jesus is inviting us here into a passionate love relationship with him that makes even our closest relationships in the world look like hate in comparison. That's why he also said in Matthew 10, "Whoever loves father or mother more than me is not worthy of me, and whoever loves son or daughter more than me is not worthy of me" (verse 37).

This brings us to the heart of what it means to be a Christian. Christianity is extreme obsession with God made possible by the gospel of Jesus Christ.

Lesser Loves

Yet I can't help concluding that such obsession is largely missing among us—and even foreign to us. Instead of God being the consuming *addiction* in our lives (the one thing we want), we seem content to make God a convenient *addition* to our lives (along with many other things we want). In our country, we've created a kind of Christianity where we've simply added God to all sorts of other people and things we love.

We love family, friends, health, work, money, success, sex, sports, exercise, food, and a host of other things in this world. Of course, we believe in God, and we say we worship him. But do we want God more than we want family or friends? Do we want God more than we want comfort or success? Do we want God more than we want money or possessions or any number of pleasures in this world? Do we want God more than we want to be liked? Do we want time with God more than we want sleep or exercise or a host of other things that fill our busy schedules? Do we want the Word of God more than we want food every day?

Even asking the questions above may cause us to wonder, *Is it bad that I love my family? Is it bad that I actually love them a lot? That I would die for them? Or for that matter, is it wrong to enjoy comfort, success, money, possessions, pleasures, a good reputation, sleep, exercise, food, and a host of other good things God gives?*

The Bible answers these questions on the whole with a resounding *no*. In the words of 1 Timothy 6:17, God "richly provides us with everything to enjoy." It's biblically right to love your family and friends, to be willing to die for other people, and to enjoy all kinds of good gifts that come from God's hand.

But here we arrive at a potential problem. If we're not careful, we can receive and enjoy these good gifts in such a way that we begin to love them more than we love the God who gives them to us. In fact, I would take this one step further. It's dangerously possible for every one of us to love family, health, hobbies, possessions, or pleasures in this world—and to even sincerely thank God for these things—*but not to actually love God.*

What do I mean?

Picture yourself alone at sea in a storm. Your tiny boat is rapidly taking on water, and you know you're about to drown. Then over the waves you see a large ship steaming toward you. It settles next to your tiny boat, and the crew hoists you out of the water. Wouldn't you be relieved?

Yet stop and ask, Does feeling grateful for your rescue by ship mean you now love the captain of that ship? Maybe. But maybe not.

You see, it's possible to love rescue without actually loving the rescuer.

I believe this scenario describes what so many people in my country call Christianity today. A host of people don't want to go to hell and will gladly take a supposed lifeboat to heaven. But when you look at our lives, it's questionable whether we actually want the One who saves us. We don't spend a lot of time with him. We don't meditate on his Word. We rarely talk about him with others. Apparently, it's possible for us to gratefully enjoy all kinds of good things and even thank God for them, but when it comes down to it, our hearts aren't really for the Giver. Our hearts are for the gifts.

And loving and desiring gifts more than the Giver isn't Christianity. It's idolatry.

A Question of the Heart

So why are our hearts like this, and how can we experience love for the Giver over and above his gifts? God's Word answers these questions in ways that are both clear and counterintuitive. In other words, God has spoken plainly in a way that goes against the way we're wired.

Look at the introduction of Psalm 63, which we've already referenced, and you'll read, "A Psalm of David, when he was in the wilderness of Judah." We don't know the exact setting David was in when he wrote these words, but most biblical scholars believe that he was on the run during his son Absalom's rebellion. Whether that's true or not, we know David was in a dark place, deprived of many of the gifts he once enjoyed: comfort, prosperity, a good reputation, community with his family and God's people, and the security that's found in all these things. He was physically in danger of death at the hands of "those who seek to destroy my life" (verse 9). In other words, David was desperate.

But not in the way that we in the United States are wired to think of desperation. So often when we're in "the wilderness," we're desperate for *things* that we're missing, whether comfort, prosperity, a good reputation, or any number of other good things. Or maybe even justice after we've been harmed. And when you peruse a variety of David's prayers in the Bible, you realize it's certainly not wrong to want or ask for these things.

But David knew that, more than needing something, he needed *Someone*. That's what is so remarkable about his response in this wilderness. Instead of longing for all sorts of good gifts, David expressed a longing for God himself. Listen again to Psalm 63:

Earnestly I seek *you*—not your gifts.
My soul thirsts for *you*—not your gifts.
My flesh faints for *you*—I just want you!
I've looked upon *you;* I've seen *you;* I cling to *you;* I think about *you* all night; my soul is satisfied in *you.*

What is better than all God's gifts put together is God himself.

Paul knew this too. When he wrote the book of Philippians, a book in which he put his passion to be with Jesus on full display, he was in jail. Deprived of all kinds of good gifts, including his freedom, he wrote, "I have learned in whatever situation I am to be content. . . . In any and every circumstance, I have learned the secret of facing plenty and hunger, abundance and need" (4:11–12). What's the secret? Communion with Christ, "who strengthens me" (verse 13). According to Paul, there is strength and satisfaction to be found in Jesus alone that far surpasses any gifts he gives (or doesn't give).

In fact, right before Paul wrote about this secret, he listed specific good gifts he'd had in this world: a good family, social status, positions of leadership and influence, and a great reputation. As he sat in that jail cell, so many of these good gifts were gone. But instead of longing for those things, he said they were like "rubbish" (literally, he said they were like dung!) compared with one thing: knowing Jesus (3:5–10). Paul actually believed that Jesus was infinitely better than all these good gifts put together.

Let's go back to our questions, then. First, why do our hearts long for gifts over and above the Giver? Could it be that we aren't seeing how truly satisfying God is? This seems to be at the root of the first sin in the world. Adam and Eve chose a gift—a piece of fruit and all the good things they thought it would bring—over God. They lost sight of who God is and the overflowing, infinite satisfaction God desired to give them in himself. And ever since that day, we've all lost sight of the same thing.

But scan through Psalm 63, and notice how David was overwhelmed by the goodness, glory, and power of the God whose love is better than life itself. Read through Philippians, and see the astonishing portrait Paul painted of Jesus as the fountain of never-ending joy, the well of otherworldly peace, the source of supernatural strength, the definition of true love, and the author of eternal life. Of course David and Paul wanted God over and above gifts in this world: They knew who God is, and they actually believed he alone was sufficient to satisfy them.

In the end, the reason we want gifts more than the Giver is that we have too high a view of gifts and too low a view of God. When I think about the best things in my life in this world, including my family and friends, I quickly realize, as great as my wife is, she's not the author of eternal life. She's not the source of supernatural strength. And she, my kids, my extended family, my friends, my church, my career, my house, my reputation, and everything else I have in this world don't even begin to compare with the glory, power, and love of God. God really is infinitely better, and he really does want to satisfy me with himself.

That leads to our second question: How do we experience this kind of love and longing for the Giver over and above his gifts? Surely the answer isn't "Try harder!" I don't think we need books or sermons or any other messages telling us,

"You should love and long for God; now do it!" After all, I don't love my wife simply because someone tells me I should (though God does tell me to love her). I love my wife because . . . well, I could write another book listing all the reasons. Because I enjoy being with her and she enjoys being with me. Because I cherish her and she cherishes me. Because we share so many of the same values, we've experienced so many of the same memories, and she makes me a better person in so many ways. You don't have to tell me that I should try hard to love my wife, because my heart finds such pleasure in who she is and how she loves me.

So if we're going to experience love for God that is greater than any other love, we don't need to *try harder;* we need *new hearts.* We need a fundamental transformation at the core of who we are. We need God in his grace to open our eyes in a fresh way (or maybe for the first time) to see how indescribably wonderful and absolutely desirable he is. To recognize how much he loves us, how much he loves being with us, and how lovely he is to be with. And to realize how much we've spurned him and sought satisfaction in the things of this world over and above him.

In other words, we need to repent. And when I say "repent," I don't just mean saying "I'm sorry." I mean we need the kind of repentance that only God's Spirit can produce deep within our hearts. We need to fall on our knees— individually and together in our churches—and cry out to God, honestly confessing everything we value, desire, or love more than him, including family, friends, comfort, sex, success, money, possessions, pleasures, power, reputation, sleep, exercise, food, or, in the end, life itself. We need to seek God as the sole end of our souls' longings with faith that, in all his glory, power, and steadfast love, he really is better than every good gift in this world combined.

A Confession

I'll be the first to admit this need for repentance in my own life. When it comes to desiring gifts over God, I am the chief of sinners. I have a frightening ability to use God as a means to an end in my life.

I think about a long season of my life after I wrote the book *Radical,* which I referenced in the introduction. That book was selling a lot of copies, and I was traveling across the country and around the world to speak at various events. The church I pastored was growing. I was loving it, working hard, and experiencing all kinds of exciting things in the church. On the outside, everything looked so great.

But during this long season, my time alone with God was basically nonexistent. Sure, I would pray in a worship service I was leading, but I would hardly ever meet with God alone. I studied the Bible in order to preach it but almost never just to know God.

That scares me. I could be successful in the eyes of the church and the Christian culture around me without any real desire for Christ. Jesus had so easily become a means to an end for me. I was using him to build an exciting church, a popular ministry, and a good name for myself. I was using God to get what I wanted in my life and in the church. But I didn't actually want God.

How sick is that?

By God's grace, he brought me to a point of repentance. He opened my eyes to so many ways I was pursuing his gifts over and above him. That led to a host of changes in my life, starting first and foremost with concentrated time with God each morning that by his grace has never abated over time and has grown sweeter literally every single day.

Interestingly, as I look back on those days, everything seems reversed in the present. Recent days have resulted in greater challenges, more criticism, less popularity, and a lot of mud slung on my reputation. This season has been one of the most difficult seasons of my life. But I can honestly say that by God's grace I am experiencing deeper intimacy with him than ever before.

And do you know what I've found? He is better. Better than I knew before. In fact, on a recent date night, I told Heather, "These have been really hard days. But I know God more, I love God more, and I am enjoying closer communion with God than I ever have. I guess if God is the goal, then these are great days."

The good news is that God is the goal. God is the end of the gospel. God is the one we need more than anything else in this world, no matter how good the gift is.

Leave Behind the Mercenary

This is what makes the gospel so great. God has made a way for you and me to be fully satisfied in him, no matter what we have (or don't have) in this world. God has sent his Son, Jesus, to pay the price for sin on a cross, to rise from the grave in victory over death, to ascend into heaven, and to declare to all who trust in him, "Not only will I save you from your sin; I will also satisfy your soul with myself. I will restore your communion with me as your Creator."

This is the biblical gospel, and we desperately need to believe and experience it today. I don't know all the trials and hurts you've walked through, though I will assume you have experienced far more difficult days than I have. But in the middle of difficulty, the biblical gospel declares to all of us that there is Someone who is better than all the best things of this world put together and that he is utterly sufficient for our souls' desires.

In this way, the gospel of Jesus is fundamentally different from an American gospel that says, "Come to God, and get [fill in the blank]." We fill in the blank with social position, political power, national pride, or personal comfort. Or maybe we fill in the blank with forgiveness, a free pass out of hell, and guaranteed entrance into heaven. But those who hear the biblical gospel hear a different invitation: "Come to God, and get God."

And this true gospel invitation to seek God as our sole purpose and greatest prize is *the* antidote we *most* need for the ideology that's poisoned the church in recent days.

Amid all the rifts in the church, we desperately need to seek the One who alone can reconcile us.

Surrounded by injustice and slander, we desperately need to seek the righteous Protector who promises to defend us and who ultimately defines us.

Immersed in politics and power plays in our country and the church, we desperately need to seek the omnipotent King who always wields his authority for good.

In the face of scandals, sexual abuse, and subsequent cover-ups, we desperately need to seek the Leader who will never let us down and the Judge, Healer, and Redeemer who will make all things right.

In other words, the one thing we most need is to behold and be with and speak to and rest in God himself. We need to seek God and God alone as the supernatural spring of satisfaction this world can't steal, grace this world can't grasp, peace this world can't take, and hope this world can't shake.

When we realize this, we can begin to understand that even challenges in this cultural moment can be a surprising instrument in the hands of a sovereign God who loves us so much that he will mercifully wean us off lesser things so that we can experience the fullness of life in him. Thomas À Kempis, medieval author of *The Imitation of Christ,* wrote,

> Do not those who always seek consolation [i.e., good gifts from God] deserve to be called mercenaries? Do not those who always think of their own profit and gain prove that they love themselves rather than Christ? Where can a man be found who desires to serve God for nothing?[1]

A few paragraphs later, Thomas wrote, "No one, however, is more wealthy than such a man; no one is more powerful, no one freer than he who knows how to leave all things . . ." and "love Jesus for his own sake."[2]

If we want this in our life—if we want Jesus *as* our life—we must leave behind mercenary religion. Let's trade in all its false promises of ultimate satisfaction in gifts, and let's step into the wealth, power, and freedom that are found in repenting of all lesser loves and running to the God whose love is better than life.

A VAST HARMONY OF SOUND AND SPIRIT

This kind of repentance is what started the movement of God that now marks the church in South Korea. The year was 1907, and the Korean peninsula was less than 1 percent Christian. The church was reeling from persecution and marginalization. Church leaders, church members, and missionaries were discouraged and divided. They needed God, and they knew it.

A group of about 1,500 Christians came together to seek God in Pyongyang (now the capital of North Korea), and God met with them in a way no one could have manufactured or imagined. During the first night of their gathering, church leaders were suddenly overcome by their sinfulness and need for God's grace. They started confessing specific sins publicly, including all sorts of hidden sins and sins against one another. A wave of similar confessions swept across the room, and people spontaneously stood to offer prayers of repentance with cries for mercy from God.

Many people were now praying aloud at the same time. One leader recorded the scene this way:

> The effect was indescribable—not confusion, but a vast harmony of sound and spirit, a mingling together of souls moved by an irresistible impulse of prayer. The prayer sounded to me like the falling of many waters, an ocean of prayer beating against God's throne. . . . [God] came to us in Pyongyang that night with the sound of weeping. As the prayer continued, a spirit of heaviness and sorrow for sin came down upon the audience.

Over on one side, someone began to weep, and in a moment the whole audience was weeping.[3]

He then quoted another person's account:

Man after man would rise, confess his sins, break down and weep, and then throw himself to the floor and beat the floor with his fists in perfect agony of conviction. [One man] tried to make a confession, broke down in the midst of it, and cried to me across the room: "Pastor, tell me, is there any hope for me, can I be forgiven?" and then he threw himself to the floor and wept and wept, and almost screamed in agony. Sometimes after a confession, the whole audience would break out in audible prayer, and the effect of that audience of hundreds of men praying together in audible prayer was something indescribable. Again, after another confession, they would break out in uncontrollable weeping, and we would all weep, we could not help it. And so the meeting went on until two o'clock a.m., with confession and weeping and praying.[4]

What had begun as a simple gathering turned into a full-on revival. It continued the next day and the next and the next. Finally these Christians scattered into village after village and church after church, where similar scenes continued. People gathered early every morning just to pray. They prayed all night on Fridays. Christians were experiencing unity in Christ, multitudes of people were coming to Christ, and churches were being planted across the country.

This move of God's Spirit didn't stop. Year after year, decade after decade, it continued among people who kept seeking God. Fast-forward one hundred years. Today there are more than ten million Christians in South Korea alone, in addition to an unknown number of persecuted sisters and brothers in North Korea. Today South Korea sends more missionaries around the world than any other country besides the United States, which is pretty remarkable when you realize South Korea is roughly the size of Indiana.

Stop and feel the weight of that.

Imagine a country today that is less than 1 percent Christian, like Afghanistan. Can you imagine more than ten million followers of Jesus in Afghanistan a hundred years from now? Can you imagine Afghanistan sending missionaries around the world with the gospel? Such a story is clearly not beyond the ability of our God.

If God did this on the Korean peninsula and if God can do this in Afghanistan, then surely God can heal the hearts of struggling Christians in our own country if we will just seek him. Early and late. Individually and together. Earnestly and continually. With confession on our lips, repentance in our lives, and loud cries of desperation for him. All together, seeking God alone, period.

SEEKING THE GOD WHO IS GREATER

I have a lot of hope that this can happen.

When I came back from South Korea, I called our church to an all-night prayer gathering. We started at eight in the evening and prayed together until close to six the next morning. It was nothing short of awesome: praising God together, confessing sin to and with one another, thanking God for his unexplainable mercy, and interceding for our church, our city, and the nations. Though we don't do this every week, late-night or all-night prayer gatherings have become my favorite moments in the church. One of my biggest regrets as a follower of Jesus is that it took me forty years to experience them—or, more appropriately, him—in this way.

Our church still has a long way to go, but I'm thankful for how others, especially in the next generation, are setting the example for us. I just returned from a two-day trip with a group of hundreds of eighteen-, nineteen-, and twenty-year-olds who are spending six months in intensive training on what it means to follow Jesus. When I arrived on the first night, I witnessed an outdoor gathering where these students spent two hours lifting their hands and voices in worship and falling on their knees and faces in prayer.

The next morning, they came together for an hour to do the same thing. All across their assembly, they prayed for different nations by name—for God's glory to be made known in all of them. That afternoon, they gathered for another two hours for the same purpose. They came together later that night to do it all over again.

Those students are spending three to five hours a day together just seeking God in worship and praying for the church here and in all nations. To borrow language from Psalm 27, they're obsessed with gazing on the beauty of the Lord and inquiring in his temple (verse 4). I don't think I've ever been around a group of students in my country who are so hungry for God. They're seeking him like he's the *one thing* they want, because they realize this is what it means to be a follower of Jesus: to believe that God is better than everything else in this world put together.

And that's the point, isn't it? God *is* better.

God is better than family and friends.

God is better than personal comfort.

God is better than people's applause.

God is better than more possessions.

God is better than social status.

God is better than political power.

God is better than economic prosperity.

God is better than [fill in the blank with anything!].

Of course, not every Christian can gather three to five hours a day with other Christians to seek God in prayer and worship. But all who believe that God is truly this good, this great, and this glorious will seek him with obsessive, addictive passion and serve him no matter what that means for our lives.

More than that, all who believe that God is this good will find ultimate satisfaction in him. Even when we have so many other good things in abundance. And even if (or ultimately when) every other good thing is gone.

7

WORTH IT ALL

Six Steps to a Different Future

Travel back with me to the top floor of the Museum of the Bible.

Look with me out across the Washington, D.C., skyline. Behold the seat of the United States government. The Supreme Court, the Capitol Dome, the White House, and all those distinguished monuments dotting the landscape in an arena of power that entices our imagination and evokes our admiration. Before our eyes lies the heart of one of the most prosperous countries to ever exist in the world.

Ironically, however, the building where we are sitting tells quite a different story. Beneath our feet lies a tribute to a book written thousands of years ago that many in our country consider antiquated and irrelevant. Yet this book claims to possess far greater power and offer far more prosperity than everything we see before us. And the contrast between these two paths to power and prosperity couldn't be any starker.

In the capital city of the world's superpower, the path to power and prosperity is paved with self-determination and self-promotion. James Truslow Adams is credited with coining the phrase *the American dream,* describing it as "a dream . . . in which each man and each woman shall be able to attain to the fullest stature of which they are innately capable, and be recognized by others for what they are."[1] In this light, the American gospel claims that anyone can make much of themselves and be seen by others accordingly.

In the Bible, however, we find that the path to true power and prosperity is actually paved with self-hatred. Jesus made that clear in John 12:25: "Whoever loves his life loses it, and whoever hates his life in this world will keep it for eternal life." These words obviously don't mean that Jesus is calling us to minimize the beauty of what it means to be made in the image of God, but in light of how that image has been marred in each of us, Jesus's initial call is an invitation to deny ourselves and take up not a dream but a cross. The biblical gospel is a clear call for all of us to crucify ourselves.

I hope that it's abundantly clear that the American gospel and the gospel of Jesus are two fundamentally different invitations. We can't choose both, and the church today is filled with the wreckage from those who've tried. And that brings us to the options before us:

- Either we unite as the bride of Christ around the gospel of Christ and the authority of his Word, or we unite as a social club around our country's ideals and our personal positions.

- Either we bridge the ethnic divide that Christ has abolished, or we deepen this divide that our country has perpetuated.
- Either we elevate God's truth or our thoughts as supreme, and either we share God's truth with compassion, or we repel the next generation.
- Either we spend our lives doing justice and loving mercy, or we spend endless hours debating justice and ignoring mercy.
- Either we reach the unreached with passion to make disciples of all nations, or we ignore the unreached with passion to make our lives in our nation great.
- Either we pursue God as the prize of our lives now and forever, or we prostitute God for prizes that will all fade.

An American gospel accompanied by a casual, comfortable Christian spin on the American dream leads to Christ-defaming division in the church and damnation for the nations, as well as the next generation. But a biblical gospel characterized by selfless, sacrificial, risk-taking obedience to the Great Commandments and Great Commission leads to Christ-exalting unity in the church and salvation for the next generation and all nations.

I invite you to embrace the biblical gospel in your life and in your church. But where should we begin? Consider six steps that I believe can be a starting point for shaking free from the vestiges of an American gospel and stepping into the fullness of the biblical gospel. I don't presume that these six steps are exhaustive, but I believe that they are a helpful beginning for moving together into a better future as followers of Jesus in our country.

1. CULTIVATE COMMUNITY ON EARTH AS IT IS IN HEAVEN

When we get to heaven by God's grace, we're going to be with a lot of people of different ethnicities who had different convictions while they were on earth and who were from different generations. So why are we waiting until heaven to experience divinely designed community, especially when Jesus made it possible for us (and called us to enjoy it) here on earth?

Part of the effect of the American gospel on our hearts is a dangerously pervasive individualism in our lives. While we've seen that there's sufficient reason for disillusionment with the contemporary church, we need to realize that the solution isn't isolation from the church. It's resolve to be the church that God has created us to be—an otherworldly family united around Jesus.

Let's commit ourselves, then, to a local church, and let's cultivate gospel-shaped community with the members of that church. One of the priorities for members of our church is involvement in what we call a "church group," which is basically a group of brothers and sisters in Christ who are committed to caring for one another like family, growing together in Christ, and making disciples together in the world. When possible, we encourage these groups to include people (1) from different ethnicities, (2) with varied personal positions and convictions, and (3) from multiple generations.

When one of these factors isn't present in a particular group, we encourage church members to intentionally cultivate that kind of community outside their church group. Ultimately, we don't want to spend our Christian lives around only people who look like us, think like us, or are in our age group or stage of life.

I'm not sure how to best integrate this into your life or church, but I would encourage you to start by considering those three categories. I realize this might look different for churches in different contexts, but to the extent possible in our communities and cities, let's work toward churches that reflect the kind of unity in diversity that we see in the Bible.

Before moving on to the next step, I should add that fostering community like this will likely not be easy. Be prepared for challenges. The whole reason we're commanded to bear with one another is that we're supposed to be around people who we struggle to bear with (and who struggle to bear with us). There are fifty-eight other "one another" commands for Christian community in Scripture, so go out of your way to obey them all, including commands to listen to one another, encourage one another, believe the best about one another, please one another, lay aside preferences for one another, and forgive one another.

Biblical community is challenging, but there really isn't anything like the church anywhere else this side of eternity. People from all sorts of backgrounds with all sorts of perspectives caring for one another like family, growing closer to God, and working together to spread the greatest news in the world among all the nations. Start by cultivating community on earth as it is in heaven.

2. SEEK GOD EARLY, LATE, AND LONG

If the *one thing* we most need moving forward is to cry out in desperation for God alone as the prize of our lives and of our churches, then we need to seek him early, late, and long. If you don't already have daily time set aside just to be with God alone in prayer and his Word, start there. If possible, make this a concentrated, extended amount of time to commune with him—sing to him, pray to him, listen to him, and sometimes just sit in silence before him. Rise early, set aside time during the day, and/or stay up late. Regardless of when, this one practice of unhurried, uninterrupted time with God will not just revolutionize your spiritual life; it will revolutionize your entire life.

But don't just do this individually. Do it collectively, understanding that there is unique reward to be found when we seek God together. Ideally, seek God like this with the people you're pursuing biblical community alongside. Gather with your entire church for extended times of prayer. If or when that's not possible, gather with a smaller group within your church. Maybe set aside a regular morning time to pray together around God's Word for at least an hour, if not more. Or maybe set aside a particular evening time—on a Friday night, for instance—to pray together around God's Word for several hours. Make it a priority to take part in an all-night prayer gathering.

As you spend extended time with God, seek him in different ways with different postures. Stand, sit, kneel, sing, shout, and sometimes just be silent. Read God's Word and pray according to it, praising him, confessing sin, crying out for your needs, and interceding for others. It might be a completely spontaneous prayer and worship time, or carefully planned. Regardless, let the Holy Spirit lead you into deep, active communion with God. (Even as I write that, I'm freshly overwhelmed with this privilege we have. Who are we to be able to commune with God? Let's steward this privilege to the full!)

Years ago, I heard someone say, "God does not reveal the intimate things of his heart to those who casually come and go." These words have stuck with me ever since, and I've found them to be true, especially since I've been a part of longer prayer times alone and with others. There is an intimacy with God that can be experienced only after seeking him for hour after hour after hour, and we're missing out if we're not willing to spend that kind of time with him. So set aside time alone and with others just to seek God. Early, late, and long. Not as a means to any other end, but as the end.

3. MEMORIZE A CHAPTER OR BOOK FROM GOD'S WORD

Seeking God involves saturating your mind with God's Word and nurturing compassionate conviction in your heart around it—much like we saw in Bashir, Moska, and other persecuted sisters and brothers. Like them, we need to trust and treasure God's Word over and above everything, including our thoughts, our country's ideals, our political positions, and popular trends. And I know of no better way to let God's Word transform the way we think than to hide large portions of it in our minds and hearts through memorization.

Now you might think, *I don't memorize well,* and that

may be true. I trust that God has given us all different mea-
sures of grace in different ways, and memorization may not
be your strength. But consider this question: If I promised to
give you a thousand dollars for every verse you could memorize between now and this time tomorrow, would you at least
give it a try? I'm guessing you would, and unless you have
unusual challenges with memory, with the promise of thousands of dollars on the table, you could probably memorize
a good number of verses.

In light of my hypothetical thousand-dollar challenge,
consider Psalm 119:72: "The law of your mouth is better to
me than thousands of gold and silver pieces." The real question isn't whether you can memorize. The real question is
whether money or God's Word itself is more valuable to you.
Or maybe another way to put that question is this: Are you
willing to seek God's Word only if it's a means to some end,
like money? Or is God's Word worthy enough in your esti-
mation to be the end?

The Bible is a treasure that is worthy of our lives, so let's
dedicate our lives to knowing it. I hope that you have a pattern of reading, studying, and meditating on it each day, but
I'd like to challenge you to go beyond that. I'm not asking
you to memorize the whole Bible in the original languages,
but couldn't you commit a chapter of the Bible to memory?

I suggest choosing a chapter from a letter in the New Testament, like Philippians 1 or James 1 or Romans 8. Try to
memorize at least one verse every few days, and keep adding
verses until you've hidden the chapter away in your heart. Or
you could spend some concentrated time one day (like an
hour or two) and see how many verses you can memorize.
Then review the verses each day until you're able to get more

concentrated time on another day. Different people memorize in different ways, so figure out what works best for you, and stick with it.

Consider asking at least one other person to do this with you so that you can encourage and help each other along the way. In addition, talk about what you're learning as God's Word is becoming a part of you. Then, after you've finished one chapter, why stop there? Keep going. Keep going until you finish an entire book of the Bible.

As I write, I'm thinking about a man in our church who took up this challenge as we memorized 1 John 1 as a church family. He had never memorized a chapter of Scripture before, and he went all in. He invited his teenage son to join in the journey, and they did it together, spending a portion of their morning car ride working on the next verse or reviewing previous verses.

After they finished the first chapter, his son looked at him and said, "We're not stopping, are we?"

His dad said, "I guess not," and they kept going all the way until they memorized the entire book of 1 John. Words can't describe the effect of this journey on this dad, his son, and their relationship with each other and with God. What could be more valuable for a parent and child to do together than to hide God's Word in their hearts?

This kind of memorization should be normal for people who treasure God's Word above all else. Put aside the constant barrage of worldly messages you're receiving, and spend time meditating on and memorizing God's Word. Make this common in your life. Start with a chapter of the Bible; then add to it as you draw closer to God. And along the way, let God's Word transform the very way you think.[2]

4. SHOW COUNTERCULTURAL COMPASSION IN THE WORLD

At the end of chapter 3, I asked a series of questions about our posture toward those who may not be Christians or may hold opinions very different from ours. Many of the people I listed are likely to have had negative interactions with Christians, or at least to have a negative impression of the church. They might include more liberal members of school boards, abortion rights activists, Muslims or others from different religions, members of the LGBTQ community, or members of the opposing political party who differ from you on just about every possible position. And I could list many others.

It's time we show countercultural compassion to those who don't agree with us. It's time we show them that the Word of God is not a weapon we wield against them but rather words that move us to show love and kindness to them. Toward this end, I want to encourage you to do three specific things in relationship with at least one person who might expect Christians to be hostile toward them:

1. Share life. Get to know them on a personal level, genuinely becoming a good friend to them. Listen to their struggles. Learn about their perspective. Seek to understand their story. Assume the best about them. Along the way, to the extent to which they are open, share your life with them in similar ways.

2. Show compassion. Go out of your way to care well for them. Not with any other motive than to be a reflection of God's love in their life. Just as Jesus taught us, love them as yourself.

3. Speak the gospel to them out of genuine love for them. As a reminder, here is a summary of the gospel:

> The gospel is the good news that the just and gracious Creator of the universe has looked on hopelessly sinful men and women and has sent his Son, Jesus, God in the flesh, to bear his judgment against sin on the cross and to show his power over sin in his resurrection so that anyone in any nation who turns from their sin and themselves and trusts in Jesus as Savior and Lord can be forgiven of their sin and reconciled to God for all of eternity.

Speak this truth at some point in your relationship with them. Pray that their eyes would be opened to the truth and beauty of Jesus and his love for them, and pray for an opportunity to lead them to life in him.

Share life, show compassion, and speak the gospel. Allow these actions to become a pattern in your everyday interactions and relationships with others who might have misconceptions about Jesus because of their interactions with Christians. Do all these things with steadfast conviction grounded in God's Word coupled with kindness and compassion toward everyone (yes, everyone) in the world.

5. DO JUSTICE

In chapter 4, I listed different ways of doing justice (though that list isn't comprehensive) and challenged all of us to hold orphans in our arms, help widows in our communities, provide for the poor in our cities, serve refugees in our country, host immigrants in our homes, rescue slaves from traffickers, visit people in prison, care for victims of abuse, come alongside moms and dads with unwanted pregnancies, and do multitudes of other things that are right for people as exemplified in God's character and expressed in God's Word.

With this as a starting place, spend time praising God for how he is currently enabling you to do justice in the world around you by the power of his Spirit. Then pray and consider one, two, or three specific additional ways that God might be leading you to do justice as an individual, as a family, or as a church. Maybe God is calling you to foster or adopt. Maybe he is leading you to help widows, single parents, children in the womb, or refugees. Maybe God is leading you to learn more about factors that are contributing to poverty or crime in a particular community so that you can be a part of helping people in that community. I could go on and on with examples, which is kind of the point: There is a lot of justice to be done in this fallen world.

Along the way, make sure to share and discuss what God is leading you to do with others in your church family. God may be leading them to join or help you. Or you may spur them on to consider unique ways he is leading them to do justice. Remember to consider how you can promote justice individually as well as through various systems and structures around you.

Just last week, our church family celebrated God's grace in Matt, a seventy-six-year-old retired Marine general who started a furniture ministry for people in need. Matt takes calls from county social workers and the abused women's shelter nearby, and he recruits people from the church to supply gently used furniture to families (usually single moms and their kids). He recently met a woman with five- and three-year-old kids who were sleeping on the floor. Matt told them he'd bring them bunk beds, and the kids asked, "What are those?"

Matt smiled and said, "Just wait and see."

The next day, the kids watched with wide eyes as this retired Marine general put together their new bunk beds, and the five-year-old shouted excitedly to his three-year-old brother, "Isn't God great?"

Around the same time, a Muslim woman who had been abused by her husband, kicked out of her home, and turned away from her local mosque was connected with Matt. Matt supplied her with new furniture, one of the women in our church family shared the gospel with her, and the woman came to faith in Jesus.

Truly following Jesus means intentionally doing justice. So take specific steps in your life, including working with others, to do justice, love mercy, and walk humbly with God.

6. REACH THE UNREACHED

God has given you a unique and significant part to play in the spread of the gospel among all the nations, so this final step involves making a plan to ensure you don't miss out on his purpose for your life. I encourage you to intentionally live out biblical passion for unreached nations by answering three questions (and the last one has two parts, so I guess it's technically four):

1. How will you *pray* for unreached nations? Come up with a plan for making time to pray for people who have never

heard the gospel. Consider how to make time to pray as a family and with others in your church. Use the daily *Pray the Word* podcast to help you pray for the unreached. Look up online resources like Stratus.Earth to learn about the spiritual and physical needs of different nations, and use the videos and prayer points included. Or download the Joshua Project app, called Unreached of the Day, and make it your pattern at some point in your day to pray for the spread of the gospel to specific people groups. The more you learn about what God is doing in the world and meet people who are going around the world, the more you'll be equipped to join with God through your prayers. Don't underestimate for a moment the part you can play in God's global purpose from your knees.

2. How will you *give* to unreached nations? In chapter 5, we explored the need to rectify the great imbalance by giving to the spread of the gospel among the least reached people in the world. Many avenues exist for you to give individually or as a church either to indigenous Christians working in unreached areas or to missionaries who leave their homes to go to the unreached. Explore Urgent (urgentneeds.org), the initiative of Radical that I mentioned earlier that identifies indigenous sisters and brothers who are doing biblically faithful, practically wise disciple-making and church multiplication on the front lines of the most urgent spiritual and physical needs in the world. Through Urgent, we come alongside these believers and provide financial support, spiritual encouragement, ongoing ministry training, and connection with

other like-minded workers. Urgent workers are remarkable (they include Bashir and Moska), and you, your family, or your church can help support the work they're doing. But you don't have to give through Urgent. Find any avenue that will help rectify this great imbalance, and let's give until the Great Commission is complete.

3. How will you *go* to unreached nations? This question has two parts because I want to encourage you to think about *where you live* as well as *wherever God leads.*

First answer, How will you go to unreached nations *where you live*? As we saw in chapter 5, God has brought people from unreached nations to our communities and cities. For example, Somali people are significantly unreached in Somalia, yet God has brought many Somalis to the United States. So look for opportunities to share the gospel with them as well as all people from other unreached people groups that God has brought near to us.

Then answer, How will you go to unreached nations *wherever God leads*? More than 3.2 billion people won't be reached with the gospel if we all stay where we live. At some point, somebody needs to go to them, and that somebody could be you. Or me.

I encourage you, then, to pray on a regular basis, saying, "God, if you want me to go to the unreached, I will go." Then, as you pray, at least think through the ways God could lead you to go. Could you go on a short-term mission trip to share the gospel among the unreached? Could you spend a summer, a semester, or a year or two among the unreached? Could you become a full-time missionary? Could you go to school somewhere among the unreached? Could you pursue job opportunities among the unreached? Could you retire among the unreached? Could you use technology in creative ways to reach the unreached? Explore all these options with the counsel of others in your church, and be open to how God could lead you to take that step at any moment. Maybe he will, and maybe he won't. But be ready at all times to go, starting *where you live* and being open to *wherever God leads*.

To be a follower of Jesus is to be consumed with God and his global purpose. If this is who we are, then let's talk about this all the time in the church, and let's be intentional—both individually and collectively—to reach the unreached.

DON'T HOLD BACK

At the beginning of this book, I shared how there is so much more to Jesus and the church than the American gospel can offer. I proposed that we can experience the awe-filled wonder of Jesus and the otherworldly beauty of his church but, in order to do so, some things will need to be different, starting not in other people but in you and me.

So here we sit, and the choice is before us. The American gospel or the biblical gospel. Worldly division or otherworldly unity. Homogeneous community or multiethnic beauty. Twisting God's Word or trusting it. Repelling coming generations or reaching them. Talking about justice and missing the good life or doing justice and experiencing the good life. Zeal for our nation alone or zeal for all nations on earth, particularly those who still haven't even heard the gospel. God as a means or God as the end. Worldly power and fading prosperity as we promote ourselves or heavenly power and everlasting prosperity as we crucify ourselves.

Let's embrace the biblical gospel. And let's do so with the sober realization that challenges will come. I don't know what all this means for you or me. But regardless of what it may cost us, let's experience and share the needed healing, guaranteed hope, unshakable joy, unexplainable unity, inexpressible love, and everlasting life that are found in Jesus alone as a part of his church.

I may not be sitting across a table from you with the Capitol outside the window, but I want to close with this gentle encouragement for you:

> With the true gospel in your heart and with God as your prize, press on, and don't hold back.

ACKNOWLEDGMENTS

I have nothing good apart from God's grace, and anything good in this book is evidence of his grace in and through so many people.

I thank God for all the encouragement, counsel, wisdom, patience, guidance, trust, and support from everyone in the publishing process, including the entire Waterbrook and Multnomah team. I thank God especially for Seth and Dave. What can I say to summarize my gratitude and affection for both of you? You are masters of your craft, and it is thrilling to be your student. And on a far deeper and more meaningful level, it is humbling to be your friend. Thank you for your investment not just in this book but in me.

I thank God for the sisters and brothers in my church family, with whom I have the unmerited privilege of serving Jesus. Amid the challenges of these days, let's keep our eyes fixed on Jesus, our chief Shepherd, and let's not hold back from becoming the church he is calling us to be for his glory among the nations, beginning in greater Washington, D.C.

I thank God for Chris and the entire and ever-growing team at Radical, and for all the ways you are pressing forward to equip Christians, serve churches, and reach the unreached. Chris, you are a friend like no other; and team, you are risk-takers who refuse to let obstacles stand in your way. Let's not hold back until women and men from every tribe, language, people, and nation are enjoying and exalting God as followers of Jesus.

I thank God for my precious wife and amazing children. Amid the challenges of these last couple of years in our family and in the church, you have trusted God and loved me at every turn. I am the most blessed husband and dad in the world, and I love you with an affection that I could never express in words. Let's not hold back from doing all that God calls us to do individually and together so that his ways are known on earth and his salvation among all nations (Psalm 67:1–2).

Most of all, I thank God for the gospel. I shudder to think of where I would be (and should be) without God's grace in my life through Jesus. May the fruit of your grace toward me resound to your glory alone through me (John 3:30).

NOTES

CHAPTER 1: FAMILY REIMAGINED

1. Bob Smietana, "Many Churchgoers Want to Worship with People Who Share Their Politics," Lifeway Research, August 23, 2018, https://lifewayresearch.com/2018/08/23/many-churchgoers-want-to-worship-with-people-who-share-their-politics.

2. David Platt, "United by Hope—Part 6, Exalting Jesus in an Election," McLean Bible Church, October 25, 2020, https://radical-net-assets.s3.amazonaws.com/images/20201030093403/MBC-102520-Platt-United-By-Hope-6-Exalting-Jesus-in-an-Election-1.pdf.

CHAPTER 2: FOLLOWING CHRIST IN MULTICOLOR

1. James W. Loewen, *Lies Across America: What Our Historic Sites Get Wrong* (New York: Touchstone, 2000), 262.

2. C. Helen Plane, quoted in Atlanta History Center, *A Condensed History of the Stone Mountain Carving* (Atlanta, Ga.: Atlanta Historical Society, 2017), 6, www.atlantahistorycenter.com/app/uploads/2021/01/Condensed

-history-of-Stone-Mountain.pdf. The following foot-note appears for this quote: Helen Plane to Gutzon Borglum, December 17, 1915, Helen Plane Papers. Special Collections Department, Robert W. Woodruff Library, Emory University, Atlanta, Georgia.

3.　Claire Barrett, "Nation's Largest Confederate Memorial, Stone Mountain, to Get New Exhibit Explaining the Site's 'Whole Story,'" HistoryNet, May 25, 2021, www.historynet.com/nations-largest-confederate-memorial-stone-mountain-to-get-new-exhibit-explaining-the-sites-whole-story.

4.　Introduction to J. H. Thornwell, *The Rights and the Duties of Masters* (Charleston, S.C.: Walker & James, 1850), iii.

5.　Thornwell, *The Rights and the Duties of Masters,* 14.

6.　Morton H. Smith, "The Racial Problem Facing America," *Presbyterian Guardian,* October 1964, 127, https://opc.org/cfh/guardian/Volume_33/1964-10.pdf.

7.　Martin Luther King, Jr., "I Have a Dream" (speech, March on Washington, Washington, D.C., August 28, 1963), www.npr.org/2010/01/18/122701268/i-have-a-dream-speech-in-its-entirety.

8.　"Unemployment Rate and Employment-Population Ratio Vary by Race and Ethnicity," U.S. Bureau of Labor Statistics, January 13, 2017, www.bls.gov/opub/ted/2017/unemployment-rate-and-employment-population-ratio-vary-by-race-and-ethnicity.htm; "Labor Force Statistics from the Current Population Survey," U.S. Bureau of Labor Statistics, January 20, 2022, www.bls.gov/cps/cpsaat05.htm; "Unemployment Rates by Race and Ethnicity, 2010," U.S. Bureau of

Labor Statistics, October 5, 2011, www.bls.gov/opub
/ted/2011/ted_20111005_data.htm.

9. Aditya Aladangady and Akila Forde, "Wealth Inequal-
ity and the Racial Wealth Gap," Board of Governors of
the Federal Reserve System, October 22, 2021, www.fed
eralreserve.gov/econres/notes/feds-notes/wealth
-inequality-and-the-racial-wealth-gap-20211022.htm.

10. "Infant Mortality," Centers for Disease Control and Prevention, June 22, 2022, www.cdc.gov/reproductivehealth
/maternalinfanthealth/infantmortality.htm.

11. "Meeting the Challenges of Measuring and Preventing
Maternal Mortality in the United States," Centers for
Disease Control and Prevention, February 28, 2018,
www.cdc.gov/grand-rounds/pp/2017/20171114
-maternal-mortality.html.

12. Nada Hassanein, "Young Black Men and Teens Are
Killed by Guns Twenty Times More Than Their White
Counterparts, CDC Data Shows," *USA Today*, February
23, 2021, www.usatoday.com/story/news/health/2021/02
/23/young-black-men-teens-made-up-more-than-third
-2019-gun-homicides/4559929001.

13. Samuel R. Gross, Maurice Possley, and Klara Stephens,
Race and Wrongful Convictions in the United States (Ir-
vine, Calif.: National Registry of Exonerations, 2017),
ii, www.law.umich.edu/special/exoneration/Documents
/Race_and_Wrongful_Convictions.pdf.

14. "K-12 Disparity Facts and Statistics," UNCF, https://
uncf.org/pages/k-12-disparity-facts-and-stats; "Labor
Force Characteristics by Race and Ethnicity, 2018," U.S.
Bureau of Labor Statistics, October 2019, www.bls.gov
/opub/reports/race-and-ethnicity/2018/home.htm;

Sandra Feder, "Stanford Professor's Study Finds Gentrification Disproportionately Affects Minorities," Stanford News, December 1, 2020, https://news.stanford.edu/2020/12/01/gentrification-disproportionately-affects-minorities.

15. Michael O. Emerson and Christian Smith, *Divided by Faith: Evangelical Religion and the Problem of Race in America* (New York: Oxford University Press, 2001), 16.

16. Korie Little Edwards, "The Multiethnic Church Movement Hasn't Lived Up to Its Promise," *Christianity Today,* February 16, 2021, www.christianitytoday.com/ct/2021/march/race-diversity-multiethnic-church-movement-promise.html; Brandon C. Martinez and Kevin D. Dougherty, "Race, Belonging, and Participation in Religious Congregations," *Journal for the Scientific Study of Religion* 52, no. 4 (December 2013): 713–32, https://onlinelibrary.wiley.com/doi/10.1111/jssr.12073.

17. Stephen Menendian, Samir Gambhir, and Arthur Gailes, "The Roots of Structural Racism Project: Twenty-First Century Racial Residential Segregation in the United States," Othering & Belonging Institute, University of California, Berkeley, June 21, 2021, https://belonging.berkeley.edu/roots-structural-racism.

18. Martin Luther King, Jr., "Letter from Birmingham Jail," April 16, 1963, https://library.samford.edu/special/treasures/2013/graphics/SC4630wm.pdf.

19. King, "Letter from Birmingham Jail."

20. Michelle Boorstein et al., "Faith Community Takes Center Stage As Thousands Again Gather for 10th Day of Protests in D.C.," *The Washington Post,* June 7, 2020,

www.washingtonpost.com/local/crowds-gather-near
-white-house-for-10th-day-of-protests-in-dc/2020/06/07
/bc924062-a6cb-11ea-bb20-ebf0921f3bbd_story.html.

CHAPTER 3: A PEOPLE OF COMPASSIONATE CONVICTION

1. Barna Group, *State of the Bible 2016* (New York: American Bible Society, 2016), 32, https://1s712.americanbible.org/state-of-the-bible/stateofthebible/State_of_the_bible-2016.pdf.

2. I taught an extensive sermon series on the topic titled "Scripture and Authority in an Age of Skepticism," available at Radical.net. At the end of that teaching, I recommended a variety of resources, including *The Enduring Authority of the Christian Scriptures* edited by D. A. Carson (Eerdmans, 2016); *Can I Trust the Bible?* by R. C. Sproul (Reformation Trust, 2017); and *Defending Inerrancy: Affirming the Accuracy of Scripture for a New Generation* by Norman Geisler and William Roach (Baker Books, 2011).

3. To learn more about Jesus's view on Scripture, I recommend reading *Christ and the Bible, Third Edition* by John Wenham (Wipf & Stock, 2009).

4. Blaise Pascal, *Pascal's Pensées* (New York: Dutton, 1958), 163.

5. Martin Luther, quoted in David M. Whitford, "Luther's Political Encounters," in *The Cambridge Companion to Martin Luther*, ed. Donald K. McKim (Cambridge, U.K.: Cambridge University Press, 2003), 182.

6. Martin Luther (Sermon, Wittenberg, Germany, March

10, 1522), in *Sermons,* vol. 1, ed. and trans. John W. Doberstein, Luther's Works 51 (Philadelphia: Fortress, 1959), 77.

7. Martin Luther, "On the Jews and Their Lies," in *The Christian in Society,* vol. 4, ed. Franklin Sherman, Luther's Works 47 (Philadelphia: Fortress, 1971), 167, 268–69.

8. Frederick Douglass, *Narrative of the Life of Frederick Douglass: An American Slave* (New York: Signet Classics, 2005), 66–67.

9. Douglass, *Narrative of the Life,* 67–68.

CHAPTER 4: OVERFLOWING JUSTICE

1. The ministry that Naomi and Dr. Zee started is called Orphan Care Ethiopia.

2. Biblical justice involves both doing right and rectifying wrong. For example, in marriage, it is unjust for a husband to oppress or abuse his wife. Therefore, justice includes stopping a husband from mistreating his wife and helping a wife who is being mistreated. Justice also includes a husband loving and serving his wife, because that is what God has said is right. Similarly, justice is both removing corrupt leaders and leading with integrity. Justice is providing education and resources for the poor to prevent sex trafficking, intercepting children who are being trafficked, and arresting their traffickers. Justice is both promoting the value of life in the womb according to Psalm 139 and working for legislation that protects children in the womb.

3. Just because someone has an advantage doesn't mean

that they should feel guilt or shame for that advantage or that they have done something wrong to gain that advantage. Maybe they have or maybe they haven't; maybe someone else has or maybe no one else has. The pictures in these scriptures involve stewarding abundance for the sake of people in need.

4. As clarification, the passage in Luke involving Zacchaeus illustrates personal restitution for wrongs Zacchaeus had done (albeit as a part of a corrupt system of tax collecting). I include it here to show how followers of Jesus in the New Testament desire to restore those who have been wronged, much as God commanded his people to do in the Old Testament.

5. The U.N. Refugee Agency notes that "89.3 million people worldwide were forcibly displaced at the end of 2021 as a result of persecution, conflict, violence, human rights violations or events seriously disturbing public order." See "Figures at a Glance," The U.N. Refugee Agency, June 16, 2022, www.unhcr.org/en-us/figures-at -a-glance.html.

6. Hannah Hartig, "Republicans Turn More Negative Toward Refugees as Number Admitted to U.S. Plummets," Pew Research Center, May 24, 2018, www.pewre search.org/fact-tank/2018/05/24/republicans-turn-more -negative-toward-refugees-as-number-admitted-to-u-s -plummets.

7. Andrea Palpant Dilley, "The Surprising Discovery About Those Colonialist, Proselytizing Missionaries," *Christianity Today*, January 8, 2014, www.christianitytoday .com/ct/2014/january-february/world-missionaries -made.html.

CHAPTER 5: RECTIFYING THE GREAT IMBALANCE

1. "Global Summary," Joshua Project, https://joshuapro ject.net.

2. Because of a variety of factors (security concerns, inconsistent reporting, etc.), it is difficult to be certain or overly precise about worldwide data related to missions and giving. This number is based on data available as of March 2020 from Joshua Project; "Status of Global Christianity, 2022," Center for the Study of Global Christianity, Gordon-Conwell Theological Seminary, last visited September 12, 2022, www.gordonconwell .edu/center-for-global-christianity/wp-content/uploads /sites/13/2022/01/Status-of-Global-Christianity-2022 .pdf; David B. Barrett and Todd M. Johnson, *World Christian Trends AD 30—AD 2200: Interpreting the Annual Christian Megacensus* (Pasadena, Calif.: William Carey Library, 2013); Jason Mandryk, *Operation World: The Definitive Prayer Guide to Every Nation,* 7th ed. (Downers Grove, Ill.: IVP Books, 2010); Todd M. Johnson and Gina A. Zurlo, *World Christian Encyclopedia,* 3rd ed. (Edinburgh: Edinburgh University Press, 2019); Todd M. Johnson and Kenneth R. Ross, eds., *Atlas of Global Christianity* (Edinburgh: Edinburgh University Press, 2009). For more on this, visit https://radical.net/secret_church/secret-church-21-the -great-imbalance.

3. If you have questions about what the Bible teaches about what happens to people who die without hearing the gospel, go to Radical.net and search there for resources on what happens to people who never hear the gospel. Or see chapter 7 in my book *Radical: Taking*

Back Your Faith from the American Dream (Multnomah, 2010).

4. John Piper, *Let the Nations Be Glad!: The Supremacy of
God in Missions* (Grand Rapids, Mich.: Baker, 1993), 46.

CHAPTER 6: GOD OUR OBSESSION

1. Thomas À Kempis, *The Imitation of Christ* (Nashville,
Tenn.: B&H, 2017), 103.
2. Kempis, *The Imitation of Christ,* 103–4.
3. William Blair and Bruce Hunt, *The Korean Pentecost
and the Sufferings Which Followed* (Edinburgh: Banner
of Truth, 1977), 71–72.
4. Blair and Hunt, *Korean Pentecost,* 72.

CHAPTER 7: WORTH IT ALL

1. James Truslow Adams, *The Epic of America* (Boston:
Little, Brown, 1931), 404.
2. For help in memorizing Scripture, I highly recommend
An Approach to Extended Memorization of Scripture
by Andrew M. Davis (Ambassador International, 2014).

ABOUT THE AUTHOR

David Platt is the author of three *New York Times* bestsellers, including *Radical*. He is a pastor in metro Washington, D.C., and founder of Radical Inc., an organization that equips Christians to be on mission from where they live to the ends of the earth. Platt received his master of divinity (MDiv), master of theology (ThM), and doctor of philosophy (PhD) from New Orleans Baptist Theological Seminary. He lives in metro D.C. with his wife and their children.

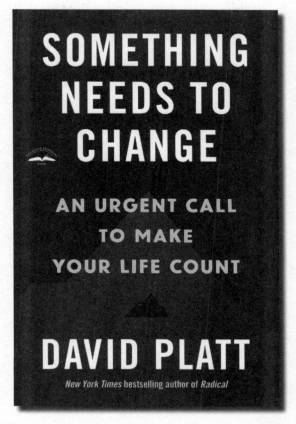

GOOD

NEWS

IS

ON

THE

WAY

 URGENT

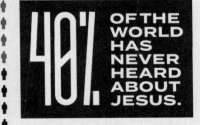

Radical's Urgent Initiative funds the high-stakes work of indigenous-led evangelism, discipleship, humanitarian aid, leadership, and church development in areas with the most urgent spiritual and physical needs on the planet.

 give today

Radical.net/Urgent